CHOOSING YOUR OTHER HALF

MARRIAGE TIPS FOR MUSLIM SINGLES

NAIELAH ACKBARALI ANAS SILLWOOD

Choosing Your Other Half:
Tips for Muslim Singles

Author Email: info@muslimmarriagecoach.com

ISBN: 978-1-7395999-9-7 *Paperback*

Published in England by
Inspired Muslim Women Ltd
Romford, United Kingdom
Tel: +44 7 915 765 815
Email: info@inspiredmuslimwomen.com
Website: www.inspiredmuslimwomen.com

British Library Cataloguing in Publication Data.
A catalogue record for this book is also available from the British Library.

بسم الله الرحمن الرحيم

وَخَلَقْنَاكُمْ أَزْوَاجًا

And We created you in pairs.

(*al-Nabā'*, 78:8)

Transliteration Table

ARABIC LETTER	ENGLISH TRANSLITERATION	ARABIC LETTER	ENGLISH TRANSLITERATION
ء	ʾ	ض	ḍ
ا	a, ā	ط	ṭ
ب	b	ظ	ẓ
ت	t	ع	ʿ, ʿa, ʿi, ʿu
ث	th	غ	gh
ج	j	ف	f
ح	ḥ	ق	q
خ	kh	ك	k
د	d	ل	l
ذ	dh	م	m
ر	r	ن	n
ز	z	و	w, ū, u
س	s	ه	h
ش	sh	ي	y, ī, I
ص	ṣ		

ARABIC SYMBOL	ENGLISH TRANSLITERATION	ENGLISH TRANSLATION
ﷺ	*ṣalla ʾLlāhu ʿalayhi wa sallam*	Allāh bless him and give him peace.
عليه السلام	*ʿalahī as-salām*	Peace be upon him.
رضي الله عنهم	*raḍiya ʾLlāhu ʿanhum*	May Allāh be pleased with them.
رضي الله عنها	*raḍiya ʾLlāhu ʿanhā*	May Allāh be pleased with her.
رضي الله عنه	*raḍiya ʾLlāhu ʿanhu*	May Allāh be pleased with him.

Table of Contents

Introduction

Is it worth it?

For many modern-day singles, marriage seems like too big of a gamble.

The risk of settling on someone, only for it to end in shambles is enough to turn anyone away from the idea of getting married. The extended hassle of choosing a spouse and the long-term struggle of creating a happy marriage just does not seem worth it anymore.

AlḥamduliLlāh, after almost two decades of marriage, we can honestly say that every second of it is worth it. Marriage is the most beautiful and most meaningful relationship that anyone can have with another human being.

In fact, most spouses have told us that a major reason they decided to marry was for the purpose of companionship. Hoping to find someone to spend the rest of one's life with is a natural desire and how Allāh Most High created human beings to feel.

Deep down inside, everyone wants to be with someone who will love them, appreciate them, and acknowledge them for who they are as a person. This applies to both men and women across the board.

From a worldly perspective, a good marriage should give you emotional stability, mental clarity, and physical fulfilment. Your spouse is meant to be your best friend, your pillar of support, and your outlet for lawful relations.

But a Muslim marriage creates something even more unique: a spiritual union between two souls. Marriage in Islam is a form of worship to Allāh Most High, and a path to Paradise for those who succeed in it.

The Prophet ﷺ said:

> **"When a person gets married, he has completed half of his religion, so let him fear Allāh with regard to the other half."**
>
> (*al-Bayhaqī*)

In this narration, the Prophet ﷺ is teaching believers that a person's religion cannot be complete without both halves.

By saying that marriage involves half of a person's *dīn*, he ﷺ is encouraging all believers in the most emphatic way to get married, while also warning them in the strongest terms to not become lax in their practice of their religion thereafter.

The type of person you marry and how you treat your future spouse is included in this Prophetic saying. Yet, nowadays, you hardly hear people advising singles on how to choose a good spouse and how to be a good spouse in return.

As a consequence, due to their lack of awareness and inexperience about married life, some singles choose the wrong person to be their lifelong partner, or they enter their marriages without knowing how to make their relationship successful.

We want to help make the transition from being single to being married easier for you. The more educated you are about married life, the better equipped you are at comfortably slipping into your role as a spouse and triumphantly producing a blissful Islamic marriage.

Through reading the advice in this book and doing the practical exercises, you will gain a better understanding about selecting a spouse and how to be a good spouse.

Step-by-step, this book will be a means for you to choose your future spouse wisely and pave the way to a successful lifelong bond together *inshā'Allāh.*

Naielah Ackbarali & Anas Sillwood
Muslim Marriage & Life Coaches

PART 1: ADJUST YOUR MINDSET

Tip #1

Admit that getting married is more important than staying single.

To stay single, or to not stay single: that is the question!

Staying single certainly has its perks.

You have a lot of individual freedom to organize your daily schedule as you see fit.

You are not troubled with the worry of taking care of a spouse's needs.

You may not have to spend a fortune on a wedding and meet all your family's cultural expectations of how it should be celebrated.

With all these benefits, why in the world would anyone want to get married?

It seems like marriage creates the opposite effect: no personal time, more problems, increased responsibilities, and a change in lifestyle.

Isn't staying single better for you?

As a matter of fact, because married life is so time-consuming, isn't it safer to do everything that you want to achieve in life FIRST, and then get married after you are through with fulfilling your personal goals?

Honestly, no.

Unfortunately, these are all false perceptions that society gives, which coax unmarried people into staying single. On top of that, hearing 'bad marriage' stories can also scare singles away from the thought of even wanting to marry in the future.

However, remaining single for too long has its repercussions, and some of which may critically impact your chances of forming a prosperous married life.

For one, living with another human being requires that you are adaptable and considerate of their circumstances. When you are younger, you are more flexible with changing your personal habits and standards. As you age, you often become set in your ways, and this attitude can lead to unnecessary marital conflict.

Secondly, all that time spent on setting out to 'conquer the world' may not provide you with the training that you need to form a lifelong bond with another person. Doing that often requires a different set of life skills that is only tried and tested after marriage.

Thirdly, purposely staying single can decrease your likelihood of getting married as time passes, which you may regret later. It could be that your pool of proposals is quite large right now, but you may soon reach a point when it shrinks or even stops.

Lastly, by deliberately choosing to stay single you are choosing to avoid the *sunna*.

Marry To Follow The Sunna

The Prophet ﷺ said, "Marriage is a part of my *sunna*, and whoever does not follow my *sunna* is not from me…" (*Ibn Mājah*, 1846)

In another narration, it is related that a group of three men came to the houses of the wives of the Prophet ﷺ asking how the Prophet ﷺ worshiped Allāh.

When they were informed about it, it was as if they deemed it little and they said, "Where are we compared to the Prophet as his past and future sins have been forgiven?"

Then one of them said, "I will offer the prayer throughout the night forever."

The other said, "I will fast throughout the year and will not miss a day."

The third said, "I will stay away from women and will never marry."

The Messenger of Allāh ﷺ came to them and said:

> **"Are you the same people who said such-and-such? By Allāh, I am more fearful of Allāh and more aware of Him than you. Yet I fast and I do not fast, and I pray and I sleep, and I marry women.**

So, whoever turns away from my way in religion *(sunna)* is not from me."

(*Bukhārī*, 5063)

The Prophet ﷺ was more fearful of Allāh Most High and more obedient to Him than anyone else in existence. If staying single was better, he would be the first to do it.

Yet, he ﷺ not only encouraged marriage, but he instructed and urged people to get married. Moreover, the previous Prophets (Allāh bless them) married. (*al-Ra'd*, 13:38)

The Rightly-Guided Caliphs – Abū Bakr, ʿUmar, ʿUthmān and ʿAlī ﷺ – married.

The commanders of armies, such as ʿAmr ibn al-ʿĀṣ, Abū ʿUbayda ibn al-Jarrāḥ, Khālid ibn al-Walīd, and Shuraḥbīl ibn Ḥasana, married ﷺ.

The same is true of most of the Companions who narrated Prophetic hadith, such as Abū Huraira, Anas ibn Mālik, ʿAbdullāh ibn ʿUmar ibn al-Khaṭṭāb, ʿAbdullāh ibn ʿAbbās, ʿAbdullāh ibn ʿAmr and others ﷺ; they all married.

Marriage is a form of worship to Allāh Most High and it is a means to becoming more devout to your Creator. It is a path to following the Prophetic guidance and an opening to grow in your *dīn*.

So why deny yourself the opportunity to develop a relationship with the *sunna* and the ability to live up to the Prophetic way?

You can tell yourself that your reasons are good, but are they any better than the *sunna*? *Alḥamduli*L*lāh*, there's only goodness and blessing in following the Prophet's noble *sunna*.

> **Marriage is a form of worship to Allāh Most High and it is a means to becoming more devout to your Creator. It is a path to following the Prophetic guidance and an opening to grow in your *dīn*.**

Marry To Stay Chaste & Contented

The Prophet ﷺ said, "O young people! Whoever among you can marry, should marry, because it helps him lower his gaze and guard his chastity, and whoever is not able to marry should fast, as fasting diminishes his sexual power." (*Bukhārī*, 5066)

Looking at the level of exposure to the types of temptations running loose in the modern world, it is obvious that Muslims are living in a time when marriage is needed more than ever as a protection.

When people decide to not marry, corruption inevitably spreads, and the risk of falling into illicit sexual intercourse or unlawful sexual behaviors is higher.

Indeed, the Prophet ﷺ said that one of the signs of the Last Day is that illicit sexual intercourse will become widespread.

Every human being has physical needs. Marriage secures your chastity and allows you to fulfill your needs in a manner that pleases Allāh Most High.

For these reasons, if you have the means to marry, it is advisable to get married as soon as possible.

It is often the case that those who delay marrying end up falling into pornography addictions, flirting with the opposite gender, becoming romantically involved with someone, or committing outright fornication (*zina*).

Unfortunately, such actions usually have a lasting impact that negatively affects your future marriage.

Marry To Have Children

The Prophet ﷺ said, "Marry the woman who is loving and fertile, for verily I shall outnumber the other nations by you." (*Abū Dāwūd*, 2050)

It is praiseworthy to have as many children as possible for Allāh Most High's sake. The Prophet ﷺ himself had seven children رضي الله عنهم.

This is one of the ultimate delights of marriage: having the chance to start your own righteous family.

By raising Godly children, you possess the power to make a difference in the world through your children. You also share in the reward for all their good actions and the generations that come forth from them.

Furthermore, your children and grandchildren will make *duʿāʾ* for you, even after you die.

By staying single, you won't be able to have your own children. Also, by delaying marriage, you decrease your chances of building a big family and giving your children siblings.

Thus, when you think about it, the perks of getting married far outnumber the benefits of staying single. So, put your doubts aside and make a firm intention to get married for the sake of Allāh Most High.

Action Steps

1. Take a moment to analyze the soundness of your reasons for staying single. Write down the reasons why you think staying single may be better for you. When you are done, leave the paper alone and take a twenty-minute break.

2. After your break, return to your list and for each reason ask:

- Is my thinking Islamic and according to the *sunna*?
- Will I regret delaying marriage if it harms my chances of getting married in the future or perhaps never marrying?
- Will marriage really stop my ability to complete my goals in life?

3. Once you are finished, now ask yourself: "So, what scares me about getting married?" Write down your answer on a sheet of paper before proceeding to the next section.

Reflections

Tip #2

Eliminate any negativity around the idea of marriage.

It's pretty worrying to think about getting married these days. With all the divorces occurring in the world, it's enough to make you wonder if happily ever after even exists anymore.

Nonetheless, routinely entertaining this doubt might influence your internal desire to marry, especially when it is coupled with a negative real-life experience.

For example, maybe you witnessed a close friend divorcing and seeing their emotional rollercoaster discouraged you from wanting to marry.

Perhaps you suffered from the detriments of a bad marriage in your own childhood home, and those wounds still hurt up to this day; consequently, you secretly vowed to never marry.

Maybe you were previously married before and your experience pushed you away from thinking about marriage again.

Now, whenever you ponder over the idea of getting married, your mind floods with negative thoughts and you get turned off from the idea. It's a recurring process that swirls around in your head, dragging you through a parade of pessimism every time you hear the word 'marriage.'

Yet, there's more to the story, and maybe more than you would like to admit. Underneath your anger is probably a very vulnerable feeling: fear.

It could be the fear of failing at married life.

It could be the fear of reliving past hurts.

It could be the fear of falling out of love.

It could be the fear of abuse.

It could be the fear of being stuck in a lifelong disappointing relationship with your future spouse.

This fear drives you to stay unmarried because you reason that it's safer to stay single. It's familiar to you, and it hasn't caused you the harm that you have seen marriages cause to others around you. It seems so logical, like the right thing to do.

But what if it's not?

What if staying single is more hurtful for you?

What if your fear is baseless?

What if you could successfully create a happy household and a blissful marriage by learning the right relationship skills?

What if your fear is really the devil in disguise whispering to you to lead you towards a way that is displeasing to Allāh Most High?

The Truth About Marriage

It may be hard for you to believe, but the truth about marriage is that its quality is based upon choices. What you do daily will create what you live in your marriage for a lifetime.

Love is a living thing. If you nurture it, it grows, but if you neglect it, it dies. Thus, happily ever after is not a fairy tale; it's a choice.

It's based on what you choose to do when feelings of dissatisfaction arise, when you don't get your way, when problems continue to resurface, and when unexpected hard times come your way.

With many 'bad' situations that you have probably heard, the individuals involved had the chance to choose too. Many of them were faced with the same choices that spouses in good marriages also face during marital upset. The difference in outcome is often a result of engaging in an advantageous or disadvantageous move.

"

Happily ever after is not a fairy tale; it's a choice. It's based on what you choose to do when feelings of dissatisfaction arise, when you don't get your way, when problems continue to resurface, and when unexpected hard times come your way.

Maintaining a hopeful outlook for your future marriage could be particularly challenging for you if you were raised in a family where your parents divorced, or they stayed married but continued to mistreat each other.

Yet, childhood wounds can heal, and they can be used as a means to grow. Many people who come from unpleasant childhood experiences have changed their lives for the better.

You can do the same. You don't have to relive anyone's mistakes. You can choose to take a different path for your own future marriage.

Divorcees may understandably be disheartened from their previous marriage experience, and some people are even put off from ever wanting to get remarried.

It is important to look at the previous marriage not as a failure, but as an opportunity to learn and grow.

Try to fairly reflect on why the marriage broke down. Use this newfound wisdom to guide you in making a more informed choice when selecting your future spouse.

Likewise, take note of what you can improve upon concerning your own character and behavior. It is often the case that those who remarry form a very happy and successful marriage because of this type of self-reflection.

Debunking Common Myths

Several relationship experts in today's times have studied common misconceptions that people generally have about what it takes to make a marriage succeed or fail. Below is a summary of four of them.

Myth #1: Conflict and anger are signs that the relationship is failing.

False.

Every marriage has fights, but happy couples choose their battles wisely. They learn how to distinguish between important issues and petty issues. In short, they get smarter about what they fight about.

Moreover, when they do fight, they control their anger, make up afterwards, and use the conflict as an opportunity to learn and grow together.

Myth #2: You are more likely to divorce if there are differences in your backgrounds, likes and dislikes, and interests.

False.

Some people think, "If I marry someone just like me, my marriage is less likely to fail." However, happy couples are sometimes very different from each other.

Yet, they appreciate their unique differences and consider the variety in styles a plus for their relationship.

As such, happy couples learn how to deal with their differences and handle the conflict that arises from it. Outside of conflict, they nurture any interests that they do share.

As a Muslim, you automatically have a common interest to nurture with your spouse once you marry, and it is Islam. You can nurture this common interest from the start.

Myth #3: In healthy marriages, spouses have the same definition of what it means to be loving.

False.

No one has the same definition of love in this world.

Real love is about understanding what it takes to make your partner feel loved and showing love based on that definition, not yours.

It's about giving to your partner, whether you agree with it or not. That's true love.

Myth #4: People just fall out of love.

False.

You need to make your marriage work. Marriage must be a priority for you. People grow apart because they're not happily sharing their lives together.

Love isn't just a feeling, it's a decision; what you decide to do daily is what makes your marriage.

The Islamic Happily Ever After

Allāh Most High says:

> **"And among His signs is that He created for you mates from among yourselves, that you may dwell in tranquility with them, and He has put love and mercy between your hearts. Verily in that are signs for those who reflect."**

(*al-Rūm*, 30:21)

If you ponder over this verse, you will notice that Allāh Most High says that He created spouses for the purpose of the two living together in tranquility.

Revelation informs you that marriage is meant to be bliss and blessing – something that brings joy and peace into your life – as it is a means for tremendous good.

An Islamic marriage is born when two strangers come together with a pure intention to create a Muslim family for the sake of Allāh Most High.

When you marry, you will swear upon the book of Allāh and the *sunna* of the Prophet ﷺ to unite with your future spouse as spiritual partners, promising your Creator that you will help each other live the *dīn* day-in and day-out.

The secret of how to achieve this sacred atmosphere in a marriage is included in the verse too. By consistently showing love and mercy towards one another, you both will create a haven for yourselves and your children; a place where you will always feel protected and secure from any outside evil.

Thus, if you want to make your future marriage a serene abode, you must make the right choices.

✔ Begin by first dealing with any lingering negative thoughts about marriage.

These gloomy beliefs will unfavorably affect your ability to choose wisely. They may influence you to overlook great qualities in a potential spouse, or they may unexpectedly trigger past trauma which holds you back from pursuing the idea of marriage.

✔ Start thinking positively about married life.

A successful marriage first starts with a promising vision. This vision must be founded upon a commitment to the virtues of hope, compassion, and selflessness.

It is from this outlook that determination is born, optimism is sustained, actions are manifest, and love bursts forth into your relationship.

“

Revelation informs you that marriage is meant to be bliss and blessing – something that brings joy and peace into your life – as it is a means for tremendous good.

Action Steps

1. For each 'bad marriage' story that you have heard, ask yourself if you really know the 100% truth about what happened in that situation. Is it fair to judge the situation if you do not?

If you were previously married, ask yourself what you would do differently in your future marriage and what type of spouse you need to help you towards that goal.

2. Reflect on your childhood experiences. Were they mainly positive or negative? Make the moves to address any past traumas or hurt that you have around the topic of marriage with a qualified therapist or counselor. The same applies to divorcees who were negatively impacted by their previous marriage.

3. Start envisioning what a successful marriage looks like.

- What do you think needs to happen for a marriage to be blissful?
- How should spouses treat each other?

Write down your dreams on a sheet of paper before proceeding to the next section.

Reflections

Tip #3

Form realistic expectations about married life.

When you enter marriage with the right expectations, married life is normally easy, joyful, and fulfilling. You are continuously inspired and driven to take care of your spouse.

Sadly, the opposite is true. Entering marriage with the wrong expectations can make married life difficult, depressing, and empty.

For some singles, their idea of what true love looks like is greatly influenced by what they see in the movies, access on social media, or read in romance novels. When their expectations are not met, they believe that something is wrong with their spouse or relationship – although it could be nothing of the sort.

When you first meet someone who you like, you may feel as if there is a unique chemistry between the two of you. Oxytocin, dopamine, and serotonin are often referred to as our "happy hormones." When you are attracted to another person, your brain releases dopamine, your serotonin levels increase, and oxytocin is produced. This causes you to feel a surge of positive emotion.

Dopamine appears at an all-time high when you are first pursuing the initial stages of a relationship with someone who sparks your interests. This high level of dopamine makes new love feel extremely rewarding, exciting, and worth pursuing over other things. You may feel like you have found your soul mate and your connection is unlike anything else.

However, the dopamine "high" eventually wears off, and you are now faced with the challenge of making your marriage work for the long term.

In almost every marriage, after the wedding party ends and the excitement wears down, real life kicks in and real faults begin to break through the veil of shiny glitter.

For some, when they see their spouse refusing to do things their way, they find themselves asking, "Who is this person that I married? I thought they were different!"

Eventually, married life does not seem that appealing anymore, especially if they keep judging their spouse and rating their marriage based on their preconceived fantasies.

If you want to avoid this type of heartache, then it is vital that you demystify any fairy tale expectations you may hold about marriage and get clued up on what married life is really like.

Fairy Tale Expectations Busted

Marriage is not a dream vacation.

Marriage is not about taking a luxurious holiday or nonstop adventure. Spouses who fall into this fantasy easily become bored with their spouses.

They start doubting the potential of their marriages too quickly because it is not as 'exciting' as it used to be. They compare their marriages to what they see on social media and think that they are missing out on something.

The truth is that for most people the newlywed stage is but a stage, and couples subsequently settle back into their normal routines. Creating enjoyable moments together takes a conscious effort thereafter, and the simpler they are, the more sustainable it will be to recreate them.

In a lifelong marriage, there will be ups and downs. There will be challenges. There will be disappointments. But there will also be heartwarming moments, good times, and triumphs. This is how life naturally is and marriage is no different.

At the heart of the matter, marriage is living real life with a real person. It is a constant test of responsibility and maturity. It is not just about what you want to do, but it's about broadening your vision to what others may want too.

Sometimes people think that 'having fun' is what will make them feel fulfilled. But it's not – the only thing that makes you truly feel fulfilled is Islam.

Thus, having contentment with your life does not come from jumping from one trend to the next, but it comes from being content with what Allāh Most High has given you in life.

Successful Muslim couples come to terms with the fact that marriage is not a teenager fling but a spiritual responsibility. They understand that creating a good marriage is a decision that stems from their maturity and the hard work they put in to make it good.

Successful Muslim couples come to terms with the fact that marriage is not a teenager fling but a spiritual responsibility.

Marriage is not a cure for unhappiness.

Your spouse cannot make you happy, they can only make you happ*ier*. If you are expecting your future spouse to continuously converse with you and spend every free moment with you, you could put more pressure on your relationship than it can bear.

Your spouse has their own problems and responsibilities outside of your relationship. You must be considerate of their circumstances. They can only give you a certain amount of time and emotional energy before they run empty on gas.

When you marry your spouse, you also marry their family, their previous life, and their problems. Likewise, your spouse will marry your family, your previous life, and your problems. Creating harmony thereafter will always bring its unique challenges.

Adopt a more balanced approach. Know that marriage is a means for you to draw nearer to Allāh Most High by way of your choices, your decisions, your attitude, and your behavior.

Rather than thinking a spouse will make you feel whole, work on strengthening your relationship with Allāh Most High and healing any open wounds *with* a qualified professional. Empower yourself by finding peace within yourself.

Marriage is not a quick fix.

Marriage is not a magic pill or a way to escape from reality. It won't fix what you have not taken the means to fix. It is idealistic to think, "Marriage will solve my problems and make me a better Muslim." That's not how it usually works.

If you have difficulties with your parents now, you will most likely still have them after marriage. If you have glitches in your character now, you will probably still have them after marriage. If you have issues with falling into the unlawful now, you may still have them after marriage.

Essentially, marriage cannot fix your personal issues, addictions, or wrong choices. If you want to resolve these issues, you must seek the appropriate help, work towards changing anything that is in your capacity, and turn to Allāh Most High for His aid.

However, at the same time, it does not mean that marriage cannot better your life. Marriage can put some of these issues into perspective, which serves as a stepping stone for overcoming them.

For example, maybe after having children you begin to realize how amazing your parents are and how much they have done for you.

Or maybe you learn how to practice patience by way of sharing your life with another human being.

Or maybe you feel so satisfied with married life that you finally feel at peace internally.

It was not your spouse that did that for you, but it was Allāh Most High who perfected your nature and fixed it.

Realistic Expectations

Realistic expectations are relationship 'wants' that are reasonable and sensible. When your marriage is characterized by realistic expectations, it is easy for both spouses to succeed in the relationship.

Realistic expectations have two defining features:

- Firstly, they are attainable by most people and are not a rare occurrence amongst couples.

- Secondly, they are sustainable in the long run and do not involve immense effort to maintain.

A few examples are:

- Mutual trust in each other.
- Equal commitment to the relationship.
- Spoken appreciation and encouragement.
- Empathy towards experiences and emotions.
- Friendship and admiration for each other.
- Satisfying sexual experiences.
- Mutual understanding and compromise.
- Respect for differences and boundaries.
- Spending regular quality time together.
- Shared acts of kindness and generosity.

In summary, if you start a marriage off with the wrong mindset, it can be a hindrance for you once problems arise. The more attached you are to those false ideals, the quicker they become excuses for why your relationship is not good enough. Adjust your mindset and hold on to what is realistic.

Action Steps

1. Relook at your answers from #3 in the previous exercise. Do you notice any unreasonable expectations based on what was mentioned in this section?

Circle them and then ask yourself: "Is this really necessary for my happiness?"

2. If the answer is 'no', cross that expectation off the list.

3. If the answer is 'yes', quickly jot down the reasons for why they are so important to you. This knowledge will help you in later sections when discussing how to know yourself better and how to choose a spouse.

Reflections

PART 2:
GET
EDUCATED
ABOUT
LOVE

Tip #4

Understand what makes a marriage successful.

When you talk to a potential spouse, it is possible that you may feel an immediate connection with them, but it's important to realize that it is not true love yet.

True love comes after marriage as your relationship develops and matures. When you learn how to live together as spiritual partners and genuine companions, this is when hearts ignite and unite.

So how do you form a successful Islamic marriage? Namely, what actions make a good marriage? The solution rests in returning to what revelation says.

Through the *Qur'ān* and the *sunna,* Muslims have been given the keys of how to make a marriage work. The *dīn* teaches that a blissful Islamic marriage is created and sustained through:

- God-consciousness
- Good character
- Gender difference appreciation

God-consciousness

God-consciousness means to be actively aware of Allāh Most High's presence such that you make Him the priority in your life. It is about staying far away from Allāh's limits so that you are always engaging in what is pleasing to Allāh Most High. It is about remembering that Allāh Most High sees and hears everything that you do, and you will be asked about it.

Making Allāh Most High your priority includes giving other people the rights that they deserve. When a person decides to marry and assume the position of a spouse, they declare their devotion to fulfilling an incumbent act of worship. Thus, living up to your role as a spouse is not an option, but rather it is an obligation.

This is why God-consciousness is key. When you try to remember Allāh Most High throughout your day and focus on the fact that He sees you, your behavior quickly changes. People act differently when they know that they are being watched.

Being conscious of Allāh Most High's presence is what will help you to consistently live up to your marital duties and motivate you to be the best spouse that you can be.

Moreover, no one can make things easy for you except Allāh Most High. When you make your intention to fulfill your marital duties for His sake, ease comes.

Actions are by intentions, and staying true to your intention to be a good spouse will put more blessings in your efforts and marriage.

When you give more to Allāh Most High, Allāh gives back to you and in ways that are indescribable. He is the

Giver of All (*al-Wahhāb*) and the Opener (*al-Fattāh*). Make your relationship with Him the foundation of your life and everything else will fall into place.

Allāh Most High says, "And whoever is mindful of Allāh, He will make their matters easy for them." (*al-Ṭalāq*, 65:4)

Good Character

From God-consciousness, what naturally follows is a desire to demonstrate gracious, good character with your spouse, in-laws, and children.

The Prophet ﷺ said:

> **"Verily, the most complete believers in faith are those who are the best in character and those who are the kindest to their families."**

(*Tirmidhī*, 2612)

According to the Prophet's noble words, all Muslims must demonstrate the strength of their faith by displaying good Islamic character. This especially holds true for spouses.

It is easy to let your guard down and stop caring about how you treat the people in your household. But it will catch up with you in the long run if you are not attentive.

Marriage is a friendship, and you cannot have a lifelong bond with someone without showing good character. If you think about what attracts you to spending time with someone, it is not because you know that they pray all night or fast every day; it is dependent upon the way that they treat you.

Everyone is drawn to someone who is warm, giving, cheerful, forgiving, patient, considerate, and loving. Thus, a spouse who focuses on demonstrating good character frequently gets what they want out of their relationship.

“

Marriage is a friendship, and you cannot have a lifelong bond with someone without showing good character.

The Prophet ﷺ said, “Nothing is heavier upon the scale of a believer on the Day of Resurrection than his good character. Verily, Allāh hates the vulgar and obscene.” (*Tirmidhī*, 2002)

Demonstrating good character matters to Allāh Most High, and it should matter to you too. Allāh does not want you to act distastefully towards your spouse. He wants you to be the best believer that you can be.

The Prophet ﷺ said:

> **"Verily a believer reaches the rank of someone who fasts all day and prays all night with his good character."**

(*Abū Dāwūd*, 4798)

Good character can be a means to increase in good deeds and enter you into Paradise. By treating your spouse nicely, you can attain the reward of a dedicated worshipper.

However, good character is not based upon your personal opinions and theories.

If you want to know what good character is, then you must look at how the Prophet ﷺ treated people. He ﷺ is your role model of how to act and react in your marriage.

He ﷺ was known to be the most gentle, loving, and caring human being to ever walk the face of the earth; consequently, he made everyone feel special.

He ﷺ was patient and kind, even when others were harsh with him.

He ﷺ would turn his body completely to face anyone who spoke to him, allowing them to feel important and heard, regardless of their social standing.

He ﷺ was generous with his time and wealth, which warmed the hearts of those around him.

He ﷺ was understanding of people's circumstances, even to the extent of shortening his own prayers for the sake of mothers with crying babies.

He ﷺ was accommodating to the concerns of others, avidly looking for ways to unite hearts and make his teachings easy to practice.

He ﷺ was easy to speak to and made himself available to the entire community, despite being a state leader, military commander, neighbor, husband, and father.

He ﷺ would tell jokes and make others smile.

He ﷺ is the true exemplar and guide of how Muslims need to interact with others. Most certainly, the blessings in a marriage come from following his ﷺ beautiful ways.

Thus, if you base your marriage on chemistry alone, you will lose because true love is not just a 'feeling' or an 'idea.'

True love is a behavior, a practice, a conscious decision, and a constant contribution.

True love is an opening for self-discovery, growth, and improvement.

True love is a shared vision for the future that you slowly work towards everyday by acting upon the principles of good Islamic character.

Good Character Qualities

- Compassionate
- Patient
- Kind
- Thoughtful
- Appreciative
- Giving
- Calm
- Easy going
- Generous
- Light-hearted
- Reliable
- Respectful
- Honest
- Loving
- Courteous
- Empathetic

Gender Difference Appreciation

Gender differences may seem like an outdated topic, but the reality is that they do exist.

Allāh Most High says, "And the male is not like the female." (*Āli 'Imrān*, 3:36)

Aside from the obvious physical differences, men and women are also dissimilar in the way that they think, communicate, and emotionally respond.

However, different does not mean that one gender is bad and the other is better. Rather, when these differences are validated and accepted, they flatter each other, especially in a romantic relationship.

It is no surprise that Islam actively encourages men to be men and women to be women since men are instinctively attracted to feminine women and women are instinctively attracted to masculine men.

This polarity in genders is what pulls each to the other, which creates the spark for lifelong passion and love.

Unfortunately, today's society is plagued with negative views around gender differences.

Men can sometimes be portrayed as abusers, narcissists, lazy, or stupid instead of smart, brave, dedicated, and warm.

Women can sometimes be portrayed as gold-diggers, selfish, bossy, and sexual objects instead of caring, compassionate, loving, and intelligent.

If you enter your marriage with these preconceived notions of the opposite gender, you may hurt your connection because you cannot see the person for who they are and what they need. Moreover, mistrust towards your spouse could form based off inaccurate perceptions.

Understanding and appreciating that men and women have different needs – instead of fighting against it – is a must for anyone who wants a happy marriage. This point will be discussed more in Tip #7.

> **“**
>
> **Different does not mean that one gender is bad and the other is better. Rather, when these differences are validated and accepted, they flatter each other, especially in a romantic relationship.**

Action Steps

1. Become more God-conscious by reminding yourself that Allāh Most High sees and hears what you do. Take note of any major sins you are committing, like missing prayers or lying. Strive to act in a way that Allāh loves.

2. Practice good character with others by trying the following:

- Be patient with others and make excuses for them, especially when they upset you.
- Be generous with your free time by lending others a helping hand.
- Be considerate of other people's feelings when making choices.

3. How would you describe men and women? Get clear on your outlook by filling in the blank for each sentence: Men are __________. Women are _________. List as many adjectives as you can.

Now analyze what you wrote. Do you notice any bias or negative views? Are your perceptions influenced by the movies or a bad childhood experience? How can you be fairer and more accurate in your assessment?

Reflections

Tip #5

Get clued up on what causes marriage problems and how to avoid them.

When you are single, it's normal to wonder what causes marriage problems and how they can be avoided in your own future marriage.

The truth is that every marriage will experience conflict and each couple will dispute about various issues at different times along their marital journey.

Just because a couple argues, it does not mean that they have a bad marriage, although it could signal that someone is unhappy with something happening in the relationship.

What separates successful couples from the rest is that they have figured out how to make conflict work for their benefit.

They embrace conflict and use it as a tool to greater serve their marital bond and personal journey in becoming better Muslims.

They treat conflict as an opportunity to connect and learn about each other's needs. In short, successful couples turn their disagreements into their allies and not their enemies.

However, a recurring number of problems are an indication that there is room for improvement in the couple's marriage. If these problems are not addressed and resolved, it can lead to the breakdown of the relationship over time.

The following is a simple overview of the top three reasons that couples experience marital problems based on our experience.

Reason #1. Not Following Revelation

Remember the keys to a blissful Islamic marriage?

- God-consciousness
- Good Islamic character
- Gender difference appreciation

When any of these ingredients goes missing, problems will brew.

Key #1 Missing: Without spouses being God-conscious, a marriage will lack in its blessing (*baraka*).

When couples commit the unlawful (*ḥarām*) by acquiring interest (*ribā*), missing prayers, or engaging in other unlawful actions, it robs their relationship of God-given success (*tawfīq*).

Moreover, by not having a strong relationship with Allāh Most High, spouses quickly lose their motivation to live up to their Islamic duties as spouses and fulfill their obligations towards each other.

Key #2 Missing: By not demonstrating good Islamic character towards each other, couples open the door to treating each other based on their emotions, instead of according to the noble *sunna*.

When you allow your emotions to drive your actions, it can easily lead to hurting the other person's feelings because you are usually not considering what you are saying or how you are saying it.

When your spouse feels criticized instead of understood, it will breed problems. In fact, the words that spouses use with each other will cultivate a certain type of culture within their relationship.

When you water your marriage with unbound criticism, contempt, and control, weeds will quickly grow over and cover the open plain of your hearts. Disagreeing turns into arguing, and fighting can transform into all-out wars.

Some people were never taught how to successfully manage their anger, and they find it normal to curse, yell, and throw tantrums. Even if you think it is okay, this type of behavior is completely wrong and when left unchecked, it can lead to destroying your marriage.

Key #3 Missing: By not appreciating gender differences, you can interpret the other person's actions the wrong way because men respond differently than women and vice versa.

Moreover, by not upholding gender differences, the relationship becomes imbalanced with too much masculine or feminine energy. If a woman is too masculine, her husband will lose his attraction for her, and the same can be said for men who are too feminine.

The solution is to follow revelation, work towards perfecting your practice of it, and make your marriage pleasing to Allāh Most High.

> **Kind words, appreciation, and tenderness are the best ways to get your needs met in a marriage.**

Reason #2. Not Meeting Each Other's Needs For Love

This can occur for several reasons.

1. <u>Communication Problems:</u> The spouse who has an unmet need is not communicating their need effectively. Perhaps they expect their spouse to mindread their thoughts or surprise them with what they want.

However, a large part of forming a successful marriage is teaching your spouse how to love you. You cannot teach if you do not speak up for yourself.

Furthermore, needs and wants must be said in a loving way – without blame, criticism, and contempt.

Kind words, appreciation, and tenderness are the best ways to get your needs met in a marriage. Thus, good communication is an essential part of any healthy marriage.

All marriages have ups and downs, but a healthy communication style can make it easier to deal with conflict, build a stronger partnership, and feel satisfied in your relationship.

<u>2. Built Up Resentment:</u> It could be that one spouse is dissatisfied with the other person's behavior or lack of action. If there is no change to the status quo, the discontented spouse's anger will grow, which inevitably breeds resentment and grudges.

As a result, the resentful spouse stops giving love and the other person starts feeling unloved. This can stimulate all types of problems in which each person feels unfulfilled and unhappy with the other.

The solution is to take your spouse's complaints seriously by listening with an open ear and an open heart.

3. Neglecting Your Friendship: Spouses need to spend time with each other on a regular basis. When you are too busy to be married, then your marriage will suffer.

The daily doses of love, appreciation, and affection can only be injected into your relationship when you make the friendship with your spouse a priority.

Dedicating some of your time to spending it with your spouse – even if it is only twenty to thirty minutes a day – can help the basic needs of love to be met.

Reason #3. Not Being On The Same Page

A lot of marriage problems stem from people's skewed perceptions. Each spouse will interpret life's events in their own specific light and this will cause them to react in a particular way.

Yet, their opinion of the situation may not even be true reality. Definitely, a person's perception can be deception.

Perceptions are greatly influenced by one's unmet expectations.

For example, if a man marries a woman expecting that she will know how to manage the household and cook, but from her point of view she never signed up to be his maid, it will cause problems.

He was expecting her to be a skilled housewife, while she was expecting something different from her wife life. Every time he asks her to learn how to cook, she refuses; in response, he thinks he's being disrespected.

The relationship turns into a rivalry of one person trying to change the other.

There are various combinations of this dynamic, and they often revolve around not being on the same page with expectations for the following issues.

1. Religion

- Which acts of worship must be performed.
- Which scholars to follow.
- Which dispensations to take.

2. Marital Roles

- Who must work and pay the bills.
- Who must cook and clean.
- Who will discipline and raise the children.

3. Lifestyle

- How clean the house needs to be.
- Where to live.
- How to spend or save money.

4. In-laws

- How to deal with in-laws during conflict.
- How much time to spend with in-laws.
- When to visit distant in-laws.

5. Children & Stepchildren

- How to raise them.
- How to discipline them.
- How to educate them.

6. Free Time

- How much time to spend on work, with family / friends, as a couple, and alone.
- How to manage phone and social media usage.
- How to spend quality time together.

7. Affection & Physical Intimacy

- What should be done outside the bedroom.
- What should be done inside the bedroom.
- Who should initiate and what is a healthy frequency.

The solution is to marry someone who shares a similar outlook as you do with these issues or to openly agree on how to handle these issues during conflict before agreeing to marry.

In order to head towards that path, you need to know yourself first and understand what has to happen for you to feel like you have a successful marriage and a good spouse.

Action Steps

1. What are your views about marital conflict? Is it a good or bad thing? Are you looking for a problem-free marriage? How realistic do you think creating that will be?

2. Exchange criticism for consideration. Try your best to understand someone's personal circumstance before criticizing them for why they didn't act the way that you wanted.

Also, if you suffer from anger problems, learn how to manage your anger with a qualified therapist.

3. Start contemplating about your future married life. Write out your preferences for each of the questions on page 55 to 57 under Reason #3.

Add any other details that come to mind which seem significant to you. Being clear on your expectations will help you when choosing a spouse.

Reflections

PART 3:
BE
REAL
WITH
YOURSELF

Tip #6

Know who you are and what you need to live a happy life.

Contrary to what many people think, the first step towards choosing your spouse is not through getting to know your potential spouse better, but rather by getting to know yourself better.

Marriage will test your personal character, individual boundaries, and level of maturity. It will sharpen your commitment to your core values, add substance to your ideals, and redefine your outlook on life.

Therefore, you need to know who you are and what you stand for FIRST.

By knowing yourself, you will be more mindful of what type of married life you want to live, what is truly important to you, what situations you can realistically handle as a spouse, and which circumstances are beyond your limit.

These are also essential details to be cognizant of when choosing a spouse. The more you know yourself, the more capable you are of explaining yourself when speaking to a potential spouse, which will help them decide if they are suitable for you too.

Knowing yourself will put your wants and needs into perspective, which will aid you in negotiating any possible conditions that must be present for you to feel content.

Moreover, it is vital that you use this time as a single to know your weak areas and strengthen them. For example, if you have anger issues, or trouble handling your emotions when hurt, or poor communication skills, then you need to work on improving them now.

This does not mean that you need to be perfect before marriage. Rather, by working on these issues now, it will help you when dealing with marital conflict, and it may even be a means to avoiding future problems.

In short, having self-awareness is crucial for anyone searching for a lifelong spouse.

Get started with the following:

1. Know your personality type.

Find out more about your personality by taking a personality test.

Even though personality tests are based on generalizations, they can give you a better indication of your overall character traits.

You can even send your results to a potential spouse or use the test's description for examples of how to explain certain qualities about yourself.

Suggested Website:

https://www.16personalities.com/free-personality-test

2. Know your love language.

Dr. Gary Chapman popularized the concept of the five love languages.

They are:

1) Receiving gifts
2) Physical touch
3) Quality time
4) Words of appreciation
5) Acts of service

A love language describes what you need from your spouse to feel loved, wanted, and accepted.

If you do not get what you need, then you think that you are 'missing' something vital from your relationship.

Take the 5 Love Language quiz online and discover your lovc languagc.

Figure out what is a 'must' for you to feel satisfied and cared for in your marriage.

Suggested Website:

https://www.5lovelanguages.com/quizzes/singles-quiz/

3. Know your personal values.

Everyone has specific preferences about the way that they need to live life to function.

These desires are based upon your unique personal values which make up your core as an individual. They influence your goals, ambitions, and outlook on life.

In fact, they are so much a part of you that if they go missing, you go missing.

Each person will have a different set of core values – including your future spouse. The aim is to understand which values matter to you the most.

By knowing your highest values, you can better gauge which areas of your life are negotiable or non-negotiable if you choose to marry someone.

Fill out the forthcoming assessment forms to determine your highest values.

1. Place a check by each statement that is absolutely important to you, meaning that it is what you need to feel happy and satisfied with your life.

2. Then, total the number of checks in each category and follow the action steps at the end.

Excelling In My Religious Practice

It is important to me to:

- ☐ Pray five times a day.
- ☐ Pray each prayer within its allocated time.
- ☐ Pray the emphasized *sunna* prayers on a daily basis.
- ☐ Pray *tahajjud, ḍuḥā*, and other *nafl* prayers on a daily basis.
- ☐ Make up any missed prayers immediately.
- ☐ Fast Ramaḍān each year.
- ☐ Make up my missed Ramaḍān fasts before the next Ramaḍān enters.
- ☐ Fast *sunna* and *nafl* fasts each year, like ʿArafāt and ʿĀshūrā', or fast Mondays and Thursdays each week.
- ☐ Pay yearly *zakāt* or give to charity.
- ☐ Intend to do *ḥajj* or *ʿumra* at least once in my lifetime.
- ☐ Eat meat that is slaughtered according to Islamic standards.
- ☐ Wear *ḥijāb* or uphold modest conduct with the opposite gender.
- ☐ Follow qualified Islamic scholarship and only take dispensations when there is a need.
- ☐ Follow the guidance of a living scholar for how to practice the *dīn*.
- ☐ Read the *Qur'ān* daily and say daily *dhikr, awrād*, and *ṣalawāt*.

Total: ____ out of 15

Demonstrating Good Islamic Character

It is important to me to:

- ☐ Be honest and trustworthy, while striving to not lie, break promises, or stretch the truth.
- ☐ Treat others with dignity and respect their honor and good name.
- ☐ Be warm and friendly to others.
- ☐ Be patient with others, apologetic, and slow to act on my anger.
- ☐ Share and be concerned about catering to other people's preferences rather than my own.
- ☐ Be avid to greet other Muslims and make polite conversation, even if I do not know them.
- ☐ Encourage others and say kind words.
- ☐ Be avid to ease the burden of another.
- ☐ Volunteer my personal time to serve and help others in need.
- ☐ Visit the sick or send food to those in need.
- ☐ Help the elderly or honor their needs first.
- ☐ Be kind and gentle towards children.
- ☐ Be generous with my guests.
- ☐ Keep good ties with my neighbors.
- ☐ Give gifts to others to connect hearts.

Total: ____ out of 15

Staying True To My Family & Culture

It is important to me to:

- ☐ Spend routine quality time with my family members or talk to them on the phone.
- ☐ Fulfill my parent's wishes in whatever they ask from me, like which career path I should pursue or who to marry.
- ☐ Serve my parents and help them with their daily needs.
- ☐ Keep close ties with my parents/siblings and share my life events with them.
- ☐ Care deeply about the way my family thinks about me and the choices I make.
- ☐ Avoid upsetting my parents/siblings at all costs.
- ☐ Live close to my family or live in the same house.
- ☐ Regularly attend family vacations or gatherings.
- ☐ Help my family members overcome their problems.
- ☐ Defend my family if they are being perceived in a negative light, mistreated, or wronged.
- ☐ Extend myself to make my family comfortable when they are around me, even if it means sacrificing my own comfort.
- ☐ Run my lifestyle according to my family's culture, like the foods I eat and how I dress.
- ☐ Marry within my family's same culture.
- ☐ Uphold my family's cultural traditions with my children.
- ☐ Have many children.

Total: ____ out of 15

Making Money & Working

It is important to me to:

- ☐ Earn enough money to live the way I like.
- ☐ Earn extra money for travel and vacations.
- ☐ Have flexibility with my money to buy higher quality items and spend as I please.
- ☐ Save money to buy a house, a car, or go on a dream vacation.
- ☐ Have enough money to buy gold or jewelry.
- ☐ Have enough money to purchase the latest phone or technology.
- ☐ Have spare cash to spend on myself or others.
- ☐ Live in convenience and ease.
- ☐ Hire others to cook and clean for me.
- ☐ Have a career and earn a living.
- ☐ Work part-time or full-time.
- ☐ Work overtime to keep my job.
- ☐ Excel in work, receive bonuses, and get promoted.
- ☐ Do what it takes to make my boss happy with my work skills and ethic.
- ☐ Dedicate myself to achieving my career goals and ambitions.

Total: ____ out of 15

Seeking Knowledge or Higher Education

It is important to me to:

- ☐ Use my free time to listen to lectures or informative programs.
- ☐ Spend my free time reading, studying, reviewing, or learning.
- ☐ Prioritize studying over other personal needs.
- ☐ Be a part-time or full-time student.
- ☐ Find enjoyment in learning and reading.
- ☐ Put in the extra effort to excel in my studies.
- ☐ Ask questions to clarify my understanding.
- ☐ Research more than what is required.
- ☐ Share what I learn with others to teach or inspire them.
- ☐ Discuss points of knowledge with other students.
- ☐ Create flexibility in my schedule to study more.
- ☐ Save my money to take a class or earn a higher degree.
- ☐ Spend my spare cash on buying more books.
- ☐ Do what it takes to make my teachers happy with me.
- ☐ Dedicate myself to achieving my study goals and ambitions.

Total: ____ out of 15

Sustaining Cleanliness, Beauty & Good Health

It is important to me to:

- ☐ Maintain a tidy household.
- ☐ Declutter disorganized areas of my house on a regular basis.
- ☐ Live in a beautiful house and/or neighborhood.
- ☐ Have access to a garden or scenic view.
- ☐ Decorate my house with trendy décor.
- ☐ Paint and refurnish my house so that it looks new.
- ☐ Smell nice and look neat.
- ☐ Dress in beautiful clothing or accessories inside or outside my home.
- ☐ Dress up for special occasions and parties.
- ☐ Buy clothes according to the latest fashion.
- ☐ Drive a nice car.
- ☐ Invest in a gym membership and exercise equipment.
- ☐ Work out on a regular basis to look good and feel healthy.
- ☐ Maintain a certain figure or weight.
- ☐ Stick to a specific diet to be healthy and look young.

Total: ____ out of 15

Maintaining Friendships & Socializing

It is important to me to:

- ☐ Spend my free time hanging out with my friends.
- ☐ Speak to my friends or message them on a regular basis.
- ☐ Keep up to date with the latest news in my friends' lives.
- ☐ Visit my friends when they return from traveling.
- ☐ Attend my friends' weddings, award ceremonies, or graduations.
- ☐ Routinely organize parties and get-togethers with my friends.
- ☐ Give back more to my friends than to my family.
- ☐ Be there for my friends when they experience difficulty.
- ☐ Go out in a group to restaurants, parks, or shopping stores.
- ☐ Participate in group trips and outings.
- ☐ Attend or organize community events and gatherings.
- ☐ Hold leadership positions or be a dedicated member for social, religious, and activist organizations.
- ☐ Host guests and invite others over to my house often, maybe even spontaneously.
- ☐ Be included in the 'loop' of being invited out with others.
- ☐ Be in people's company and spend time with others more than be alone.

Total: ____ out of 15

Action Steps

1. The categories with the highest number of checks are the values that matter to you the most. For any category that received the highest number of checks, reflect about how you can explain the importance of this value to a potential spouse.

Use phrases like:

- "It's important to me that…"
- "I really value that…"
- "In order to be happy, I'm the type of person that needs…"

2. While reading through this list of statements, did any other details come to mind that you realized are equally important to you? Write them down and include them in your explanation.

3. For the categories with lesser marks, upholding these values is probably less important to you. If any particular statement from these categories is truly important to you, add that statement to your list.

Reflections

Tip #7

Make sure you are ready to live up to the responsibility of being a spouse.

A common question that singles ask is how to know if you are ready for marriage.

The Prophet ﷺ said, "Every one of you is a shepherd and every one of you is responsible for his flock. The leader of a people is a guardian and is responsible for his subjects. A man is the guardian of his family, and he is responsible for them. A woman is the guardian of her husband's home and his children, and she is responsible for them. The servant of a man is a guardian of the property of his master, and he is responsible for it. No doubt, every one of you is a shepherd, and every one of you is responsible for his flock." (*Bukhārī*, 5188)

Marriage is a serious commitment in Islam. Out of His infinite wisdom, Allāh Most High gave each spouse rights and responsibilities, which will be asked about on the Day of Judgement. Thus, readiness for marriage basically boils down to being responsible and mature.

The Islamic framework for marriage is based upon spouses fulfilling each other's rights and living up to their designated responsibilities. This beautiful setup creates an interdependency, such that both spouses rely upon each other for love and support.

When each person is concerned about pleasing their spouse and carrying out their duties for the sake of Allāh Most High, these God-given roles work in unison together and produce harmony between the two people.

It lays a foundation for creating a happy home for their future children.

Therefore, you need to fully understand what your role will be as a husband or wife before deciding to become one.

Islamic Rights & Responsibilities

The duties of a spouse can be seen from three angles:

1) Rights of both spouses.
2) Rights of the wife only.
3) Rights of the husband only.

Rights of Both Spouses

As for the rights that relate to both spouses, each person is entitled to love, support, respect, emotional safety, physical safety, sexual fulfillment, loyalty, and fair treatment.

They should not reveal each other's secrets, especially with matters related to the bedroom unless there is a need.

Rights of the Wife

As for the rights that relate specifically to the wife, she is entitled to food, shelter, and clothing, as well as a dowry (*mahr*).

Her husband must be patient with her emotions and character. He is also required to be just in how much time he spends with her, especially if he has more than one wife.

Islamically a wife has the right to her own live quarters and privacy from in-laws.

Rights of the Husband

As for the rights that relate to the husband, he is entitled to be the final decision maker and the head of the household; this is because he assumes the role of a provider and protector over his wife and their children.

His wife is required to protect his money and honor, especially in his absence. She must not allow anyone into his house that would displease him, and she should not leave the house in a way that would upset him.

She should also nurture their young children. However, both are responsible for raising the children together and educating them about the *dīn*.

Aside from the responsibilities mentioned through revelation, spouses need to possess an emotional and social intelligence when interacting with each other. A great source of conflict can arise around gender differences.

As previously mentioned, men and women have been created differently. A common mistake is that men expect women to act and think like men, and women expect men to act and think like women.

If you want to avoid this pitfall in your marriage, then it is crucial for you to understand what love could mean for the opposite gender.

Love for a Woman

The greatest thing that a man can give a woman is his unconditional love, care, and attention. A wife wants to feel like she's a priority in her husband's life.

Love for a woman consists of:

1. Spending Quality Time Together

Women want to feel emotionally connected to their husbands. This only happens when men spend regular quality time with their wives and dedicate effort towards improving their friendship.

Quality time could be taking her out on a date, making conversation with her, or listening to her speak about her life.

Being present with her sends the message that her husband cares about her, which makes her feel super special.

2. Being Reliable

Women want to feel like they can count on their husbands for financial and emotional support.

When a man takes responsibility to financially provide for his wife and family, it increases a woman's appreciation for him in her life. She does not want to be burdened with the worry of bailing her husband out of debt or trouble.

Likewise, she needs to feel like she can rely on her husband to be a source of comfort for her, especially during the most stressful and troubling times.

A woman's trust in her husband decreases every time he runs away whenever problems arise. She wants a provider and protector in her life, and that can only happen when he shows up for her.

3. Being Generous

However, paying bills is not the only thing that she wants. A woman hopes that her husband will buy her thoughtful gifts and be willing to spend on her beyond his obligatory duties.

Gifts do not need to be expensive, just thoughtful. She wants to know that her husband is thinking of her. Taking her out on dates or family vacations is also a smart move.

4. Giving Appreciation

Women want to be noticed for their contributions, especially around the household and with raising the children. They don't want to feel like their husband expects them to be the maid, the cook, or the kids' babysitter.

A little thank you goes a long way. Whenever a husband shows consideration for the effort that his wife puts into the family, she feels cherished and adored.

5. Speaking Sweet, Soft Words

Women need men to show kindness, patience, understanding, empathy, and compassion. They expect that their husbands will frequently say loving words, call them by endearing names, and compliment their beauty.

Whenever a man habitually calls his wife cute names, it warms her heart, and whenever he consistently tells his wife that she is beautiful, it increases her confidence in herself.

Furthermore, being kind and patient at the time of responding to her emotions is a must. When she's upset, she wants to be comforted and consoled – not attacked or judged, which will only cause her to feel bad about herself.

She wants to be able to express her sadness, pain, and anguish openly and receive a shoulder to cry on, an ear to speak to, and a comforting hug of reassurance. At the heart of the matter, every woman wants her husband to be her best friend.

Love for a Man

A husband wants to feel that his wife understands his deepest essence and is driven to take care of him, just as he is naturally driven to take care of her.

Love for a man consists of:

1. Showing Him Respect

From an Islamic standpoint, all of Allāh's creatures deserve your respect.

Whether they are humans or animals, insects or rodents, males or females, white people or brown people, adult or child, Allāh Most High commands His believers to treat each of His creatures with dignity and respect.

Yet, Allāh Most High also specifically mentions and singles out husbands in revelation.

Allāh Most High says:

> **"Men are the caretakers of women, as men have been provisioned by Allāh over women and tasked with supporting them financially. And righteous women are devoutly obedient and, when alone, protective of what Allāh has entrusted them with....."**

(*al-Nisā'*, 4:34)

The derivative meaning of the Arabic word for 'caretakers' refers to taking care of, managing the affairs, and being in charge.

When scholars discuss what this entails in a marriage, they mention that Allāh Most High designated the husband to be responsible for supervising the overall household affairs and acting as the final decision maker.

However, his guardianship over his wife is not a license to oppress her, but rather, scholars warn that it is a grave religious responsibility which he will be questioned about on the Day of Judgement. His role as a caretaker is more of a burden than a claim for power.

Interestingly, when a man views his caretaker position as his God-given duty, it compels him to work hard to support his family.

It motivates him to exert himself beyond measure. It inspires him to be a good role model for his children. It gives him purpose in his life.

Consistent respect sends the message that a wife is her husband's number one fan, and it encourages him to love her, to want to be around her, and to take care of her needs.

2. Being A Supportive Friend

When a wife is her husband's friend, she is an altruistic, kind, and loving companion. Her husband feels like he can just be himself around her without the worry of thinking that he's a failure.

She's someone who admires his virtuous qualities, supports his ambitions, listens to him express his dreams or worries, believes in him, cheers him on, and demonstrates good character towards him. She is avid to lend a helping hand and offer her service. She's also positive and upbeat, not overly negative or critical.

3. Giving Appreciation

Because men have a desire to protect and provide, they're always looking for someone who appreciates these qualities in them.

Thus, they want to be actively thanked for their contributions towards the marriage, the children, and the household – no matter how insignificant they may seem to her.

This especially holds true with thanking him for his dedication towards earning a living and excelling in his career.

4. Looking Attractive

Men are visual creatures. They feel proud when their wife is pretty, and she makes a conscious effort to stay in shape and look presentable in his presence.

Her attempts to appear beautiful show that she is concerned about his opinion of her, and it registers in his mind as a sign of love.

5. Flirting & Frequent Bedroom Activity

Many people underestimate the power of the bedroom. In almost all good marriages, lovemaking occurs on a regular basis. It is natural, normal, and healthy.

Sexual fulfillment is a right of both spouses. However, it's usually the case that men have more of a sexual appetite than women.

When a wife ignores a man's need in this area, his temptation grows for what is outside the house. It is very frustrating for a man to decide to spend the rest of his life with someone, thinking that she understands him and will fulfill this basic human need, but only to end up in disappointment at her lack of attention and interest.

In a good marriage, both spouses are eager to please the other.

Action Steps

1. Review the section on Islamic rights and responsibilities. Do you believe that you are ready to live up to your designated role for the sake of Allāh Most High?

If you answered no, which duties are you unable to fulfill? How could you take the steps towards strengthening your capability?

2. Review the explanation for what love is for a man and a woman. Can you notice any differences between the qualities each gender expects from the other? How would you handle these differences in your own marriage?

3. Furthermore, ponder about which good qualities you can bring to your future marriage. Why would you make a good spouse? Why should someone marry you?

Reflections

PART 4:
CHOOSE
WISELY

Tip #8

Make a distinction between musts and wants.

It is often said that marriage is a union between two imperfect people who refuse to give up on each other.

The moral of the story is that there's no such thing as a perfect spouse. Therefore, you should not demand perfection when selecting a spouse.

You need to be realistic. Searching for someone who ticks every single box that you have can be unreasonable – especially if your list of requirements is based on superficial desires rather than substantial concerns.

Instead, you need to learn how to make a distinction between 'must-have' qualities you require in a spouse and 'wants' that are possibly negotiable. By sticking to what Allāh Most High has revealed, you will be steered in the right direction of how to differentiate between the two.

Prophetic Advice

The Prophet ﷺ said:

> **"If someone comes to you whose religious commitment and character are pleasing to you, then marry (your daughter) to him. If you do not, mischief and enormous evil will spread the Earth."**

(*Tirmidhī*, 1085)

The Prophet ﷺ teaches that the most important qualities to consider when choosing a husband is the person's religious commitment and their capability to practice good Islamic character. The same wisdom also applies when choosing a wife.

Firstly, a righteous Muslim is mindful of Allāh Most High's presence and fears displeasing Him. From their God-consciousness (*taqwā*), they avoid doing things that earns Allāh's anger.

Consequently, they stray far away from lying, cheating, and abusing others. Instead, they are motivated to be just, fair, and truthful.

Secondly, a Muslim who demonstrates gracious Islamic character will act with care and speak with concern. They will avoid being rude, selfish, and inconsiderate.

Most certainly, they will strive to be virtuous, kind, and respectful. Moreover, they will raise their children with proper Islamic etiquette and morals.

Thus, possessing these two qualities is what will lay the foundation for a good relationship and ultimately lead to marital bliss.

In another narration, the Prophet ﷺ said, "A woman is married for four things: her wealth, her family status, her beauty and her religion. Marry the religious woman otherwise you will be losers." (*Bukhārī*, 5090)

This proves that a person's relationship with Allāh Most High is the golden standard when choosing a spouse.

However, being religious is not limited to praying and fasting. Rather, it's about how that person lives Islam daily.

For example, is it important for this person to follow the *Qur'ān* and the *sunna*?

Do they care about sinning?

Are they concerned about excelling in their *dīn*?

“

This proves that a person's relationship with Allāh Most High is the golden standard when choosing a spouse.

Be wary of someone who recently became religious. They may be overzealous about performing acts of worship now, but it could fizzle out after time.

In truth, a person's practice of Islam needs to be consistent over a lengthy period for it to be solid.

- ✔ Try to marry someone who has been committed to consistently practicing the *dīn* for at least a year, preferably three years.

- ✔ Furthermore, look for someone who shares a similar religious outlook and standards.

Marrying someone who does not pray while you pray five times a day will cause conflict.

Marrying someone who does not eat Islamically slaughtered meat while you only eat it will cause disagreements.

Marrying someone who does not believe the man is the final decision maker while you believe the man is the head of the household will cause issues.

Moreover, sisters should be cautious about pursuing a non-Muslim man in the hope that he will convert to Islam to marry you. Faith must be sincere for it to be accepted.

- ✔ Focus on marrying someone who has already converted, accepted the message, and is comfortable with living the *dīn*.

He will be a better example for you and your children.

It must be mentioned that there can often be pressure put upon new Muslims to quickly get married, especially for convert sisters who are quickly proposed to by those who were born Muslim.

For many cases, there are different cultural expectations of marital life and gender roles that make such marriages very difficult for new converts.

- ✔ For these reasons, we advise converts who have only recently entered Islam to wait until they have adjusted to their new faith before looking to get married.

As you grow in your practice of Islam, you will find yourself rapidly changing your perspective on people and what you want from life.

If you decide to get married now, you might end up marrying someone who you are incompatible with, which can cause unexpected hardship.

The *ḥadīth* on page 90 (*Bukhārī*, 5090) also shows that there is nothing wrong with wanting to marry someone who is attractive, wealthy, or comes from a good family.

- ✔ Being physically attracted to your spouse is necessary for an intimate relationship.

- ✔ Marrying someone who has the means to financially support you is necessary for survival.

✔ Choosing someone who will provide you with good in-laws is necessary for your mental health and future children.

By analyzing the framework provided by the Prophet ﷺ, you learn how to choose someone who will help create and sustain a lifelong marriage.

Other Qualities to Consider

On top of the Prophet's advice ﷺ, it is crucial that you only speak to someone who outwardly shows that they are ready to live up to the duty of being a spouse.

Do not waste your time with someone who is not serious about pursuing marriage.

Be on the lookout for someone who is:

1. Responsible

- From a religious angle, the person has sought their personally obligatory knowledge (*farḍ al-ʿayn*). This means they know how to pray, pay *zakāt*, fast, earn lawful money, and the like.
- They seek guidance from scholars, teachers, and the righteous on how to live an Islamic lifestyle.

- From a worldly perspective, they make good decisions with their money, time, and capabilities.

- They aren't relying on their parents or friends to always bail them out for their mistakes.

2. Reliable

- They are known to fulfill their commitments to others.

- They are dedicated enough to finish the important tasks on their plate.

- They are not carelessly jumping from one duty to the next.

3. Honest & Loyal

- They keep their promises to others.

- They keep a respectful distance with the opposite gender.

- They give straight forward answers instead of wishy-washy responses.

4. Cheerful & Easygoing

- They smile a lot and are lighthearted.
- They are not cold, controlling, pessimistic, or overly serious.

5. Able to Control Their Anger

- Their family and friends vouch that they do not blow up often.
- They don't make you feel bad about your answers, blame you for your decisions, or get angry during your interactions together.

6. Caring, Giving, & Thoughtful

- They are good to their family and friends, as well as your own.
- They treat you and your parents nicely, and they speak to you warmly.

7. Considerate & Supportive

- They agree to accommodate some of your needs or dreams.
- They seem content, impressed or pleased by your qualities.
- They are open-minded or curious about hearing your ideas and perspectives.

8. Generous with Their Time

- They say things which indicate that they want to spend quality time with their spouse and children.
- They give you as much time as you need in the meetings and do not seem like they are ready to rush off.

9. Clean & Presentable

- They care to wear clean clothes, take a shower, and look neat. They do not smell or appear slobby.

10. Healthy

- They maintain a decent weight, do not have any known diseases that would severely impact your marital life (e.g. cancers, STIs), and are mentally and emotionally stable.

- They are free from physical issues that would permanently prevent you from having children together or physical abnormalities that would impact your ability to be attracted to them – unless you are happy to marry into this situation.

Deal Breakers

The secret to creating a blissful marriage is not through getting everything you want but through making the best out of your circumstances.

As such, it is imperative that you marry someone who leads the type of life that you can handle, and you avoid marrying someone who will pull you into circumstances that will make married life difficult for you.

Yet, with so many issues to consider, how do you decide which ones take precedence when selecting a spouse?

A great way to know what cancels someone out is by having deal breakers.

Deal breakers are what are essential for you to have – or avoid – when married. Otherwise, you would not be able to happily live with the other person.

Each person will be unique in what they can tolerate. When considering your deal breakers, keep the following questions in mind.

Knowing yourself:

- What situations can you handle? What situations can you not handle?
- Which issues are you willing to negotiate or be flexible about? Which issues are you not willing to negotiate or be flexible about?
- Will you feel the same way five, ten, or twenty years from now?

Examples of deal breakers are:

- Missing prayers or not practicing.
- Living with in-laws.
- The husband does not work.
- Contributing to the household bills 50/50.
- Being a second wife, or it being a strong possibility in the future.

- Smoking cigarettes.
- Porn addiction.
- Confirmed fertility or impotency issues.
- Interacting freely with the opposite gender.
- Engaging in a long-distance relationship for a lengthy period.
- Marrying someone from abroad for their citizenship or residency.

Be on the alert for anyone who has circumstances that conflict with your deal breakers.

A few things to keep in mind:

Do **not** have more than five deal breakers. Otherwise, you may run the risk of being too picky.

Do **not** make your deal breakers too specific such that it limits you to a small percentage of people.

Do **not** base your deal breakers on superficial issues, but rather choose deal breakers that revolve around religious matters and common areas of marital conflict.

Do **not** directly tell the potential spouse that this issue is a deal breaker for you. You want to make sure that they answer honestly and are not compelled to say things to impress you.

Do **not** immediately reject a potential spouse who does not initially meet one of your deal breakers.

Unless it is obvious that you are not a good match, practice your communication skills and discuss the matter together in a meeting. Explain your reasons and listen to how they respond.

Try using phrases like:

- I cannot…Would you be willing to reconsider?
- It would be very hard for me to be in a situation where…How strongly do you feel about it?
- I want to make it clear that … is not a possibility for me. What do you think about that?

Talking about it may further clarify the matter for you. It could be that you reach a compromise, or you later realize that this issue was not a real deal breaker in the wider scheme of things.

Remember that contentment in this world does not come from receiving everything you want. Take a realistic approach and aim to marry someone who is compatible with you in the areas which are most important to you.

Action Steps

1. Make a list of qualities which you hope for in an ideal spouse, like their religious practice, character traits, educational background, age, ethnicity, country of residence, and whatever else comes to mind.

2. For each response, circle which are an **absolute must** for you and put the letter 'x' by which ones you **ideally want**. Keep the following questions in mind.

Knowing yourself:

- What situations can you handle? What situations can you not handle?
- Which issues are you willing to negotiate or be flexible about? Which issues are you not willing to negotiate or be flexible about?
- Will you feel the same way five, ten, or twenty years from now?

3. From the circled statements, pick your top five. These are your deal breakers.

Reflections

Tip #9

Ask and do not assume.

You may feel a mixture of emotions when you are trying to choose someone to marry. Depending on the situation, you could feel elated, confident, enthusiastic, nervous, overwhelmed, or doubtful.

These are normal feelings to experience when you are seeking a spouse and speaking to someone for marriage. However, it is important that you do not allow your emotions alone to direct you.

Emotions can change based on how you feel that day, and they are usually not a reliable source to depend upon when making a lifelong decision.

Instead, your common sense, gut instinct, intuition, and logic must lead the way. This will help you to make a wise choice, agree on sensible negotiations, and be cautious so that you avoid falling into unlawful interactions or other troubling situations.

Finding A Potential Spouse

It is common to hear unmarried men and women complain about the difficulty of finding an appropriate spouse, especially a religious spouse.

While it is true that there are challenges, there are many opportunities available nowadays. It is important that you seriously explore all options instead of giving up.

The five most common methods are:

1. Your Family Circle

This may seem old-fashioned, but there is still a lot of wisdom in choosing this route if it is possible for you.

Pros:

- ✓ You will be supported by your family throughout your journey.
- ✓ Your parents may have inside knowledge about other families which helps reduce some of the uncertainty that comes with getting married.
- ✓ It reduces the chances of becoming romantically involved before marriage, which can lead to illicit relations or unnecessary heartbreak.
- ✓ Parents often have wisdom about who could be a good spouse based on their life experiences.

Cons:

- ✗ Your parents might not be on the same religious page as you. So, they might suggest someone culturally appropriate from their perspective, but religiously inappropriate from your perspective.

- ✗ Your parents and family may not have a wide range of contacts.

- ✗ Your parents might unnecessarily delay things or pressure you to marry before you are ready.

2. Your Social Circle and Contacts

This includes asking anyone outside of your family, like friends, teachers, local scholars, community leaders, and marriage counselors. Let people know that you are seeking a spouse and ask if they have anyone in mind. If you attend a religious circle or religious social groups, then you might also meet likeminded people this way.

<u>Pros:</u>

- ✓ You may find someone with the same religious background and interests as yourself because they occupy the same social circles.

- ✓ You can get to know the potential spouse by either interacting with them directly or getting references from people who actually know them.

<u>Cons:</u>

- ✗ If you do not have a wide social circle or set of contacts, you might not have access to a very large pool of people.

3. Matrimonial WhatsApp Groups

This involves submitting your CV / brief profile to the WhatsApp group moderator, and you can also access the profiles of other members. Some groups facilitate and moderate meetups between interested parties.

Pros:

- ✓ If well-run and popular, these groups can widen your potential pool of partners.

- ✓ Groups that are run with the help of scholars ensure that correct Islamic boundaries are kept. They may also facilitate meetups, like through a shared Zoom meeting.

- ✓ Potential partners might be more serious and religious than those found on commercial matrimonial websites.

Cons:

- ✗ It can be difficult to discover which WhatsApp groups are available and decent enough to join.

- ✗ You will not know much about the potential spouse except what is mentioned in their profile, which is typically very basic.

4. Muslim Matrimonial Websites and Apps

Countless matrimonial websites now exist, catering to different segments of the Muslim community. Some may have a reputation for facilitating dating, but there are others that are more serious and cater to religiously oriented seekers.

Pros:

- ✓ You gain access to a very wide pool of potential partners from across the globe.
- ✓ Some websites offer helpful features, like personality compatibility screening, religious filters, chaperons, and matchmakers.

Cons:

- × You need to be very cautious because people can be deceptive or psychologically unstable. There are unfortunate stories of people who were taken advantage of by individuals with fake profiles.

  Therefore, if you want to explore this route, you must approach each person with caution, research their background thoroughly, and ask for references from their family members and friends who you can contact to ask direct questions about them. Only meet up with someone in a public space and always take a friend or relative.

- ✗ It is possible to get into a habit of looking at the opposite gender, speaking to several people at once, revealing your personal information to strangers, falling into the unlawful by using it as a means to chat rather than seriously talk for the purpose of marriage, and becoming attached to someone who is not good for you to marry.

5. Matrimonial Meetups and Conventions

Organizations facilitate group meetups where people have a chance to get to know who is there and potentially find a suitable partner.

Pros:

- ✓ Some of the meetups are targeted at specific groups – like professionals or those over 35 – enabling you to meet people more like yourself.

- ✓ It is a safe space, given that it is public and you do not meet up with the other person alone.

Cons:

- ✗ It can be very awkward to speak about yourself and then potentially be ignored or turned down.

- ✗ It is a small pool of people, and you may not find anyone to marry among the attendees.

Approaching Someone for Marriage

If you see someone you like, you can state your interest in speaking to them for the purpose of marriage through an intermediary, like a family member or friend, or you can directly approach the person too.

The first step is to find out general information about the person before agreeing to speak more seriously or meet up.

This will save you from the embarrassment of having random people know about your personal life or from the hassle of meeting more people than needed.

At this stage, inquire about their:

- Full name
- Age
- Religious practice in general
- Ethnicity and cultural background
- Height and body size
- Educational background
- Job position
- Overall mental and physical health

Some people also exchange photographs at this stage if they have not seen each other in person. Keep in mind that photographs can be deceiving.

- If you are somewhat attracted to their appearance, keep the door open. Don't reject someone just because their appearance is not exactly what you want.

- If they were previously married, you may want to know the basic reasons for the divorce and if there are any children under their care.

- Once you understand these points and are interested in knowing more about them, ask to exchange answers for questions focused more on the topic of marriage via email or a phone call.

- It is best to have a third party cc'd in your email interactions. Likewise, if you are speaking via the phone or an online meeting, have specific questions in mind so that your conversations are structured.

Examples of marriage-focused questions are:

- Why are you seeking to get married?
- What are your most important goals in life?
- What are your most important values in life?
- Which words would you use to describe your overall character?

- Name three of your top positive qualities and possible negative traits.
- What is something that you are passionate about? Why does that mean so much to you?
- Where do you see yourself five years from now? How about ten or twenty years from now?
- What role does religion play in your life? How would you define what type of Muslim you are?
- What are your expectations of married life?
- What is your vision of a happy household?
- What are you looking for in a spouse? Which traits are a must?

Do not put all your hopes into the sparks or butterflies you may experience while talking.

Instead, notice whether you feel comfortable with the person's responses to your questions, their overall character, and their general views on religion and life.

If what is shared appeals to both of you, then you should agree to meet in person in a public place or at a house where a parent/chaperon is present to ask more serious questions.

In all these situations, it is recommended that a familiar third party be nearby while you are speaking, like in another room or table at a restaurant. This will prevent you from getting too comfortable with each other, which can lead to crossing Allāh's boundaries if you are not careful.

Interacting Before Marriage

Anyone who you consider marrying remains unlawful (*ḥarām*) for you to touch or be completely alone with until you do the marriage contract (*nikāh*).

Whenever you decide to meet up, talk, or email one another, it must be for the sole intention of getting to know each other for the purpose of marriage.

This is not a license to reveal everything about yourself or act in a way that is equivalent to dating. Instead, it is an opportunity and an opening from Allāh Most High to take serious steps towards choosing a lifelong partner.

Thus, you must still behave modestly, dress like how you would in front of other *non-maḥram* individuals, and practice self-control over your desires.

There are people who lower their guard with these criteria, only to end up wounded and ashamed when things don't work out.

Save yourself from the heartache and stick to Allāh Most High's guidance on how to interact with the opposite gender. This will place more blessing and goodness in your future marriage.

Meeting the Family

Because marriage is a union between two families, it is quite common for the potential bride and groom's family to meet first before deciding to marry.

If you are in this circumstance, take care to treat the potential spouse's family members with the utmost dignity and respect. First impressions often hold weight, and any bad manners on your part may give their family a certain impression of you, which can carry over into married life.

This is also an open opportunity for you to assess their family. Take note of how they treat you and how they interact with each other. Do you feel at ease with what you can sense of the family's dynamic? Keep your eyes wide open, and do not ignore any worrying signs.

Nonetheless, even if their family situation is not what you ideally hoped for, do not automatically reject the person. Instead, take it as a chance to ask questions later on about how they would handle potential issues that may arise if you married into their family. Then, base your final judgement on what was said.

Making the Final Decision

As for how many times you should speak or meet before agreeing to marry, there is no maximum or minimum amount. You should speak and meet as many times as you need to make a sound decision.

During your time together, ask as many questions as you deem fit to fully understand and fairly assess the person's religious practice, character, personality, outlook on life, ambitions, goals, ideas of a wife's role, ideas of a husband's role, management of money, social media usage, and the like.

You should also discuss issues related to in-laws and raising a family, like expectations around how to interact with their family, past family history, how many children to have, and whatever else is important to you. A list of **over 100 suggested questions** is given on page 156.

The general rule is: ASK! DO NOT ASSUME ANYTHING. Sometimes you may need to inquire about matters that are private or somewhat embarrassing.

Don't let that discourage you from looking into issues that would give you second doubts about staying in the marriage were it to be revealed later in the relationship.

For example, even if someone describes themselves as religious, it's often relative. If you are looking for someone who practices their religion according to a specific way, then directly ask if they do those things.

Do not allow looks to deceive you; unfortunately, a person with a big beard may be the one who is struggling to wake up for *Fajr* every day.

As for being different in personality and temperament, do not let it discourage you from proceeding further. For instance, if the other person is shy to speak but you are talkative – or vice versa – it is not a sign that your marriage will be doomed. Instead, you will need to learn how to maneuver around each other's differences.

Marrying someone who shares the same temperament and personality as you will not necessarily guarantee a successful marriage. What matters is whether you are compatible in the way that you view and live out your religion and life.

More exactly, the best protection against serious marriage problems is to:

- ✓ Marry someone who is on your same page religiously.
- ✓ Select someone who does not conflict with your deal breakers.
- ✓ Openly agree on how to handle common issues that create conflict before agreeing to marry. See page 55 to 57 (Tip #5) and page 156 for ideas.

It is expected that you will be excited if things are moving in a more promising direction. However, do not allow your emotions to completely cloud your logic or invent a dreamy version of the other person that is untrue.

- ✔ Look for someone who is already what you want.
- ✔ Don't marry anyone thinking that you can change them into what you want afterwards.
- ✔ Judge the person based on what they actually say and show you. That's who they truly are and that's who they will truly be in the marriage.

Thus, when it comes to making your final decision, ask yourself these key questions:

- Can I accept this person for who they are?
- Do I feel comfortable with the thought of being married to this person for a lifetime?
- Will I be happy with this person being the father or mother of my children?

It is important that you also ask for references. You cannot rely solely on what the person tells you. Everyone puts their best foot forward when spouse seeking.

- ✔ You must inquire about their character from others, like their family, friends, or co-workers.

✔ Request that they are honest as possible because it will help you to make a good decision for your own life.

Red Flags

Red flags are signs that indicate the person probably cannot have a healthy relationship or proceeding down the road together could be emotionally dangerous.

Some examples are:

- Becoming more religious for 'your sake.'
- Lacking seriousness around religious practice, like with praying and fasting.
- Asking you to change how you practice your religion, like no longer wearing *hijab*.
- Pushing you to marry without your parents' approval or without meeting your parents.
- Being emotionally entangled with you but not taking active steps to marry you.
- Refusing to register your marriage legally or make your marriage publicly known.

- Wanting to engage in sexual intercourse or inappropriate touching before marrying you.
- Unresolved addictions to pornography, video games, alcohol, or drugs.
- Unhealed aversions or trauma around sexual intercourse.
- Growing up in a highly dysfunctional household and not taking the means to seek therapy.
- Yelling at you, being excessively argumentative, showing severe mood swings, and making you feel bad about yourself or your decisions.
- Being rude or disrespectful to your parents, family members, or friends.
- Pulling you away from your family or friends.
- Rushing to marry when you haven't asked all your questions yet.
- Brushing your questions aside, like "Don't worry, it will work out."
- Being violent or threatening in their demeanor.
- Displaying excessive arrogance, inflated ego, or denying the reality of your situation.

- Making you feel amazing and then treating you like dirt.
- Lying, hiding the truth, or being excessively secretive.
- Being abnormally controlling, jealous, or protective.
- Ghosting or ignoring you.

✔ While you are interacting with a potential spouse, be on the lookout for anything that pushes your uncertainty button or makes you feel unsafe.

✔ Trust your intuition and do not ignore obvious red flags. If a potential spouse triggers red flags, then you should not marry them.

✔ Keep checking in with yourself about whether you are comfortable to move forward or not.

✔ Weigh out the benefits and consequences of being married to this person.

In conclusion, before deciding to marry, you should ask all the questions that you need to make a good choice. Be honest with yourself and seek Allāh Most High's help in your final decision.

Action Steps

1. Think about how you would answer the **marriage-focused questions** mentioned on page 112 to 113.

Look at the **100+ Potential Spouse Questions** on page 156 to get ideas of questions to ask a potential spouse.

2. Review the list of red flags. Would you add any to the list? What would it be?

3. If you are having trouble with being picky, ask someone who is experienced with marriages to help you choose your deal breakers and guide you to decide what is most important to you.

Reflections

Tip #10

Increase the blessings in your choice.

Even if you have followed the best spouse seeking tips in the world, nothing you do will be successful without the blessing of Allāh Most High.

He is the One who bestows benefit and wards off harm. It is only through His power, His might, and His aid can you be guided to choose the best spouse.

Most certainly, Allāh Most High wants you to turn to Him and rely on Him for your outcome.

Make Du'a

The Prophet ﷺ said, "'There is no Muslim who calls upon Allāh with a supplication that does not entail sin or cutting family ties, but that Allāh will give him one of three answers: He will either quickly fulfill his supplication, or store it for him in the Hereafter, or divert an evil from him similar to it.

The Companions رضي الله عنهم said, 'In that case we will ask for more.'

The Prophet ﷺ said, 'Allāh has even more.'"

(*Aḥmad*, 11133)

By way of your supplications and prayers, Allāh Most High promises to give you the good, protect you from evil, and divert your life from harm. Thus, when seeking a spouse, making *duʿāʾ* cannot be emphasized enough.

- If you want to increase the chances of your *duʿāʾ* being answered, then be sincere while making your *duʿāʾ* and say it in a state of absolute neediness.

- Pray the prayer of need (*ṣalāt al-ḥājah*) and beg Allāh Most High to answer your need for a good spouse.

- Make *duʿāʾ* EVERY DAY for a good spouse from the time you are single until the time you marry.

- Supplicate and beg Allāh Most High during the moments when *duʿāʾ* is most likely to be answered, like within the last portion of the night at *tahajjud*.

There is no specific *duʿāʾ* related in the Qurʾān or the *sunna* for seeking a spouse. However, scholars mention that the following *duʿāʾ* can be said because a righteous spouse is from the good (*ḥasana*).

رَبَّنَا آتِنَا فِيْ الدُّنْيَا حَسَنَةً وَفِيْ الآخِرَةِ حَسَنَةً

وَقِنَا عَذَابَ النَّارِ

Rabbanā ātinā fid dunyā ḥasanatan wa fil ākhirati ḥasanatan waqinā ʿadhāb an-nār

"Our Lord, grant us what is good of this world and the Hereafter, and protect us from the punishment of the Fire."

(*al-Baqara*, 2:201)

Pray Istikhara

When considering a person for marriage, one should pray two *rakaʿāt* and say the *duʿāʾ* for seeking guidance (*istikhāra*) after the final *salām*.

You can pray the prayer of guidance as many times as you need. The more you rely on Allāh Most High to choose for you, instead of relying on yourself, the more you will find that your final choice will be blessed (*mubārak*) and have God-given success (*tawfīq*) in it.

Unlike what some people think, the answer to your *istikhāra* is not in seeing a dream.

Rather, scholars note that Allāh will either place ease in your heart or the matter you are praying for will become easy for you to do or head towards.

The existence of obstacles and difficulties could indicate that Allāh Most High does not want you to go in that direction.

Sometimes singles delude themselves with their *istikhāra*. They are already attached to the person and interpret their *istikhāra* through their emotions, even in the face of obvious red flags or hardship.

You need to turn to Allāh Most High sincerely seeking what He wants. Try your hardest to free your heart from your personal inclinations and open it up to being guided by Allāh alone.

Always remember that Allāh Most High is all-Wise and all-Knowing. He will only direct you towards what is best for you. There is nothing to lose.

Du'ā' for *Istikhāra*

اللَّهُمَّ إِنِّي أَسْتَخِيرُكَ بِعِلْمِكَ
وَأَسْتَقْدِرُكَ بِقُدْرَتِكَ وَأَسْأَلُكَ مِنْ
فَضْلِكَ الْعَظِيمِ فَإِنَّكَ تَقْدِرُ وَلَا أَقْدِرُ
وَتَعْلَمُ وَلَا أَعْلَمُ وَأَنْتَ عَلَّامُ الْغُيُوبِ

اللَّهُمَّ إِنْ كُنْتَ تَعْلَمُ أَنَّ هَذَا الْأَمْرَ
خَيْرٌ لِي فِي دِينِي وَمَعَاشِي وَعَاقِبَةِ أَمْرِي
فَاقْدُرْهُ لِي وَيَسِّرْهُ لِي ثُمَّ بَارِكْ لِي فِيهِ

وَإِنْ كُنْتَ تَعْلَمُ أَنَّ هَذَا الْأَمْرَ شَرٌّ لِي
فِي دِينِي وَمَعَاشِي وَعَاقِبَةِ أَمْرِي
فَاصْرِفْهُ عَنِّي وَاصْرِفْنِي عَنْهُ وَاقْدُرْ لِي
الْخَيْرَ حَيْثُ كَانَ ثُمَّ أَرْضِنِي به

Allāhumma innī astakhīruka bi ʿilmika wa astaqdiruka biqudratika, wa as ʾaluka min faḍlikal- ʿaẓīm fa innaka taqdiru wa lā aqdiru wa ta ʿlamu wa la a ʿlamu wa anta ʿallāmul-ghuyūb.

Allāhumma, in kunta ta ʿlamu anna hadhal-amra [mention decision here] khayrun lī fī dīnī wa ma ʿāshī wa ʿāqibati amrī faqdurhu lī wa yas-sirhu lī thumma barik lī fīhi.

Wa in kunta ta ʿlamu anna hadhal-amra sharrun lī fī dīnī wa ma ʿāshī wa ʿāqibati amri faṣrifhu ʿannī waṣrifni ʿanhu waqdur lī al-khayra haythu kāna thumma arḍīnī bih

O Allāh, verily I seek the good from You, by Your knowledge, and I seek ability from You, by Your power, and I ask You from Your immense bounty. For indeed You have power, and I am powerless; You have knowledge and I know not; You are the Knower of the unseen realms.

O Allāh, if You know that this matter (*mention what you are asking for here*) is good for me with regard to my religion, my livelihood and the end of my affair then decree it for me, facilitate it for me, and grant me blessing in it.

And if You know that this matter is not good for me with regard to my religion, my livelihood and the end of my affair then turn it away from me and me from it; and decree for me better than it, wherever it may be, and make me content with it.

Involve Your Family

Once things seem to be moving in a very serious direction and you are considering saying yes, then at this point if you have not done so already, your parents should be informed.

Out of respect for their feelings, it is important to involve them in the process at this stage, even if it is to simply ask for their opinion or blessings.

Islam does not endorse secret marriages. One of the wisdoms of inviting everyone in the community to the wedding party is for the purpose of publicly announcing that two people are uniting in a lawful manner for the sake of Allāh Most High.

There are several drawbacks when you marry behind your parents' back.

For one, your marriage may lack in blessings. It could be that the way you are going about your marriage is a form of disobedience to your parents, which is sinful in general providing that your parents do not entreat you to disbelieve in Allāh Most High or commit the unlawful.

Moreover, when your parents find out, it may incite more trouble in your life than the hassle of trying to push them harder to agree on the marriage. You will only be able to keep your marriage a secret for so long, especially if you want to have children.

Not to mention, when you marry in secret, it increases the possibility of the marriage contract being conducted in the wrong way. If you are not aware of the exact Sacred Law rulings for how to conduct an Islamic marriage contract, you may falsely marry and that has serious implications too.

However, some people have special circumstances since their parents make it very difficult for them to marry. For example, some parents may decide to reject a promising person just because they are not from their same cultural background or village.

If this is your situation, before deciding to jump into a marriage, consider any valid points from your parents' side:

- Are you honestly willing to handle the challenges that come from a cross-cultural relationship?

- When your cultures clash, whose culture will take precedence?

Whereas you may not be able to foresee any potential problems now, these conflicts often increasingly manifest after couples have children and try to raise them according to their unique cultural values and mannerisms.

Likewise, marrying in secret could set off automatic problems with your in-laws. Muslim marriages are often a marriage between two families. What type of impression will you give your in-laws by marrying in secret?

Additionally, by marrying in secret, you never give yourself the opportunity to assess the other person's family and how they could possibly treat you as a daughter-in-law or son-in-law, which is what should happen during your premarital meetings.

If you are in a situation where you do not have any other person to consider or this person is a good Muslim who can help you lead a pure Islamic life, then make sure that a righteous scholar is involved in your selection process and is able to better guide you on how to marry considering your parent's opposition.

Deal With Disappointment Wisely

It could be the case that you put all your hopes into a potential spouse, but it did not work out. Depending on how long you interacted with each other, letting go may seem difficult and painful.

1. **Give yourself time to heal.** Some situations take longer to overcome than others. Dealing with disappointment can be difficult.

2. **Release any mental pressure and breathe.** Journal your thoughts. Speak to a friend about what happened. Avoid bottling up your feelings.

3. **Process the experience and learn from it.** There is always a lesson that you can take from anything that happens to you in life. How did you grow from this situation? What would you repeat again? What would you do differently?

4. **Keep the hope alive.** Who you marry is written for you. Allāh Most High knows what is best. This may have been a step you had to climb before something better comes your way. Even the pain you feel could be a means towards expiating your sins.

The Prophet ﷺ said, "How wondrous is the affair of the believer! There is good for him in every matter, and this is not the case for anyone except for the believer. If he experiences ease, then he thanks Allāh and that is good for him, and if he experiences hardship, then he remains patient and that is good for him." (*Muslim*, 2999)

When you believe that your heart is not attached to the person anymore and your mind is clear, start searching for your other half again.

Travel the Road to a Successful Marriage

Once you have chosen your other half, it is vital that you take the means to create and sustain a successful marriage from day one.

- ✔ Make your marriage a priority, treat your spouse kindly, and treasure their companionship.
- ✔ Consider signing up for premarital coaching for expert guidance on how to transform your

relationship into a blissful, lifelong bond. See page 156 for information about our premarital program.

- ✔ Read marriage books by relationship experts and learn about what marriage entails. Attend marriage workshops and classes as a couple.

- ✔ Lastly, do good deeds together and make constant *duʿāʾ* for each other and your marriage.

One of the best prayers to say is:

رَبَّنَا هَبْ لَنَا مِنْ أَزْوَاجِنَا وَذُرِّيَّاتِنَا قُرَّةَ أَعْيُنٍ
وَاجْعَلْنَا لِلْمُتَّقِينَ إِمَامًا

Rabbanā hab lanā min azwājinā wa dhurriyyātinā qurrata ʾaʿyun wajʿalnā lil muttaqīna imāmā

"Our Lord! Bless us with pious spouses and offspring who will be the joy of our hearts and make us models for the righteous."

(*al-Furqān,* 25:74)

May Allāh Most High grant you a beautiful marriage.

Action Steps

1. If you haven't started already, begin making *duʿāʾ* for your future spouse and marriage. Make as much *duʿāʾ* as possible, especially during *tahajjud* time and other blessed occasions.

2. Pray the prayer of guidance (*istikhāra*) when considering a potential spouse.

Ask Allāh Most High to make it easy for you to make a good decision and to give you what is best for your worldly and next-worldly life.

Ask Him to show you anything that may be a future concern in the relationship and to place ease in your heart if you continue to proceed.

3. Use the forthcoming checklist on page 139 to help guide you in your decision.

Reflections

Choosing A Spouse Checklist

Whenever you are considering someone, use this checklist as a tool to assist you in making your final decision. It will help you to recall your answers from the previous exercises.

- ☐ Are you both on the same page in your religious beliefs, practice, and outlook? (Tip #8)

- ☐ Have you shared your highest values with them and what is important to you in life? Were you comfortable with their reaction to what you said? Do you know what they value the most? Are you comfortable with their values, direction, and outlook on life? (Tip #6)

- ☐ Have you discussed your views and preferences regarding religion, marital roles, lifestyle, in-laws, children, free time, and affection? Do you know their views and preferences on these matters? Have you agreed on what to do if conflict arises concerning these issues? (Tip #5, 7, & 9)

- ☐ Does anything conflict with your deal breakers? Knowing yourself, what situations can you handle? What issues are you willing to negotiate or be flexible about? Will you feel the same way five, ten, or twenty years from now? Have you expressed your boundaries regarding these issues? (Tip #8)

- ☐ Can you accept this person for who they are? Do you feel comfortable with the thought of being married to them for a lifetime? Are you happy with the thought of them being the father or mother of your children? (Tip #9)

- ☐ Have you spoken to their references to find out their opinions about this person? (Tip #9)

- ☐ Will marrying this person make married life spiritually, emotionally, physically, or financially difficult for you in any way? (Tip #9)

- ☐ Did you notice any red flags? Do you trust them? Do you feel safe with them? Does anything bother you about their circumstances? (Tip #9)

- ☐ Are you clear of any fairy tale expectations? Are you rushing into things or contemplating about what really matters? (Tip #3)

- ☐ Do your parents know that you are seriously considering this person for marriage? Have you spoken to them about it? Has this person spoken to their parents about it? (Tip #10)

- ☐ Have you assessed their family? Are you willing to marry into their family despite whatever issues may arise? Have you spoken to them about how they would handle potential problems between you and their family? (Tip #9)

- ☐ If you have children from another marriage, have you spoken about everything that concerns you with bringing your children into a new household? Have you discussed how you will manage potential custody issues, problems, or interactions with your ex-spouse?

- ☐ Have you asked all the questions that you need to make your final decision? Is there anything else left to consider for you to be certain that you want to marry this person? (Tip #9 and page 156)

- ☐ Have you prayed *istikhāra* about marrying this person? (Tip #10)

May Allāh place blessings and goodness in your final decision *inshā'Allāh.*

Common Questions

1. Why don't Muslims date? What makes Islamic matchmaking better?

It is tempting to think that dating is the best way to determine compatibility with a potential spouse. The truth is that dating does nothing of the sort.

When you date a person, you are primarily meeting up with the understanding that you are going to have fun together. It's usually done without an intentional long-term seriousness.

In fact, dating is mainly about creating short-lived experiences that make you feel good. Unfortunately, this can give you a false perception of who the person really is and what they would honestly be like in an everyday marriage. No one is 24/7 fun and in a good mood.

The other issue with dating is that it often leads to crossing Islamic boundaries between genders. Meeting up progresses into hugging, then into kissing, and possibly into something worse.

Through His infinite wisdom, Allāh Most High does not allow men and women to become physically intimate before marriage. There is so much goodness in following Allāh Most High's way.

Many people who choose to transgress these boundaries end up regretting it later. Through the pain of a broken heart when things do not successfully result in a marriage or the shame of exposing one's body to another person before marriage, dating only leads to intense regret and emotional harm.

The best way to determine compatibility is not through dating but by:

- Asking serious questions about a person's religious practice, life direction, and vision for married life.

- Investigating the person's background through their references. This should consist of a list of anyone who can attest to their true character, like family members, friends, and co-workers.

- Praying about the marriage and asking Allāh Most High for His guidance in your affair.

Culturally, this process is commonly referred to as 'Islamic matchmaking.' Even though the name may sound like someone is choosing a potential spouse for you, the reality is that you choose for yourself.

There are no forced marriages in Islam. The most someone can do is suggest a potential spouse for you. However, even if someone believes that you will be an excellent match together, you cannot rely on others to choose for you. No one knows you better than yourself. Always responsibly and sensibly explore every option suggested at your own will.

2. Can I ask about their past sins? Should I reveal my sins?

In general, you cannot ask about what past sins they fell into, nor should you reveal your own sins.

Once a sincere repentance has been made, those sins are wiped out and should not be a topic of discussion.

You should only question what could possibly impact you and your future relationship, like sins that the other person is still engaging in.

For example, acceptable things to ask about are:

- Inquiring how often a person misses their prayers and what they have done to rectify it.

- Finding out how willing they are to change their interaction with the opposite gender if there has recently been inappropriate behavior.

- Requesting to see the results of an STI test to affirm the absence of sexually transmitted infections.

However, if you know that someone had an irreligious past, you may be concerned if they really turned a new leaf. It is possible for past sins to creep back into a person's life, especially when they are placed under a lot of pressure, stress, or hardship.

If the person has shown signs of long-term change and others who know them have confirmed their changed behavior, then you may want to overlook your doubts.

If they are still new to practicing the *dīn*, then you should take your time in getting to know them, ask others about their character, and carefully assess all the facts before agreeing to marry.

Ask serious questions about where the person is right now and where they want to head.

Beg Allāh Most High to guide you in the process and reveal anything to you that could cause future issues. In short, do not marry anyone who you cannot trust.

As for advice to the person who has an irreligious past, please be honest with yourself about whether you really have stopped committing certain sins with the opposite gender, alcohol, or drugs.

Being sober for a few months is not sufficient. Rather, you need to be free from these vices for at least a year or longer.

It is not fair to seek a lifelong relationship with someone who has lived a life free of this behavior when you have not seriously stopped indulging in the unlawful.

If you return back to your previous ways, it may cause your spouse to undergo trauma and a lot of pain. It will be an injustice to them and their families to act like you will be a righteous spouse but in reality you are not ready to live up to this type of responsibility.

3. Should I ask for a high mahr?

A dowry (*mahr*) is the right of the wife. It is a gift that the husband gives to his wife after completing the marriage contract. It demonstrates the seriousness and importance of the marriage-contract, and it is a token of respect and honor to the woman.

According to some scholars, the *mahr* must minimally be ten dirhams, which is around $30 USD. There is no limit to the maximum amount.

Some women stipulate a high *mahr* because they are afraid of losing out if they got divorced in the future. Whereas this could be a concern, asking for a high *mahr* upfront may not be the way to secure yourself. It can turn away potential suitors who would be excellent husbands but do not have the financial means to provide a high *mahr*.

It is possible to ask for a certain amount upfront and delay the rest upon the event of divorce. You could also request that your *mahr* is paid in installments every year; for example, $1000 USD per year for a period of 10 years. A scholar should be consulted about how to properly stipulate this in the marriage contract.

Don't let your fears push good suitors away from you. The best guarantee against divorce is to marry someone who you are compatible with and to make the moves to be a good spouse from the start.

Do not rush into marrying anyone. Take your time getting to know the person and watch out for red flags.

4. What if my parents don't agree with who I want to marry?

If your parents don't agree with your decision, first try to understand their side. Perhaps they possess deeper insight into issues that you have not considered. It is important that you listen to what they have to say, even if you disagree. Be polite and show them respect.

Once you have heard their opinion, carefully reflect on their points. If you do not agree with what they have said, clarify your side in a gentle manner. Point out the benefits of why you think this person is best for your life. Then give them the room and time to think about it.

If they still refuse and you really believe that this person is the best person for you to marry, you may want to get a third party involved, like a close friend of your parents, a local scholar, or someone who your parents will respect. Maybe they could help your parents understand your reasons or assist you to fairly weigh out the pros/cons of your situation.

You should also frequently ask Allāh Most High to make marrying this person easy for you if it is best for your faith and worldly life. *Inshā'Allāh* if that is the case, Allāh Most High will make it manifest.

5. Should I hold off on marrying until I can afford the wedding expenses and the cost of living as a couple?

It is true that marriage ceremonies in today's times can be expensive and complicated affairs, with lavish weddings attended by countless extended family members, and a potentially significant bridal *mahr* payment.

Many men find the costs daunting, especially when they are just starting off in their careers. They must also take into consideration the monthly expenses thereafter of supporting a wife and potential family. So, it is understandable that spending a lot of money on one night can be off-putting.

But over-delaying marriage is not the solution. Rather, there needs to be a mature and open conversation between the couple and with their respective families to meet expectations in a way that is affordable and closer to the sunnah of the Prophet ﷺ.

The wedding expenses should not be excessive and the *mahr* payment should be an amount that is reasonable and not a deterrent to the couple wanting to get married.

The Prophet ﷺ said, "The best of marriage is that which is made easiest." (*Ibn Hibbān*, 4163)

In terms of how to have these conversations, the prospective couple first need to be on the same page with each other about this matter.

Then each person can speak to their own families about wanting to get married in a way that is closer to the *sunna*, which will therefore have more blessing in it.

If you haven't met anyone yet, and it is your parents who are doing the searching for you, then let them know in advance what your preferences are.

It may be hard to sit down and have this conversation with them, but if you make *duʿāʾ* and intend it for Allāh's sake, then He will bring about an opening, even if it takes some time.

6. Should porn addicts get married? How do I ask a potential spouse about a porn addiction?

Porn addiction ruins marriages in so many ways.

Erectile dysfunction, impotence, premature ejaculation, emotional withdrawal, and psychological damage are some of the issues that a couple may deal with when a spouse is a porn addict.

Both men and women can become porn addicts. If you are someone who is a porn addict, deal with your addiction BEFORE getting married. You should be sober for at least a year before considering a spouse.

Marriage will NOT solve your addiction.

From our experience, the best way to stop a porn addiction is through understanding how your addiction plays out, taking the means to stop it, and holding yourself accountable, even if it be with a coach or support group.

As for finding out if someone has an addiction, you can ask an older relative or community leader to openly talk to the potential spouse while you are not present.

Another option is that you could directly ask the potential spouse if you should be concerned about addictions to anything (e.g. images, films, video games, drugs, etc) and see what they say.

You can explicitly mention that you do not want to marry anyone who is a porn addict or even watches porn occasionally. That gives the person the opportunity to withdraw from talking to you for marriage without having to admit anything.

It may be a good idea to ask about their phone and internet usage. Do they find themselves using it a lot? What do they tend to look at? What's their view of inappropriate images?

Sisters could stipulate the right to divorce themselves upon finding out about a porn addiction. That may deter an active porn addict from pursuing the marriage. A scholar should be consulted about how to stipulate this condition in the contract.

7. How can I tell if the person is from a toxic family?

It is crucial that you understand the family dynamic of the person you will marry, especially if your in-laws may suffer from personality disorders like narcissism or borderline personality disorder (BPD).

Start by directly asking the potential suitor about their childhood. Inquire if they had a happy childhood, would they change anything about what they experienced if they could, and how close they are with their parents and siblings.

When you meet with the family, pay attention to how they speak to you. Notice how they interact with each other too. Do you sense a pleasant atmosphere in their home? Does it seem tense, fake, or creepy? If something seems off, trust your instincts.

If you still want to consider this person, then it may be wise to ask them about what you noticed, but in a way that does not attack or insult their family. Find out what role you will need to play to keep things peaceful.

If you are able, you can also ask others in the surrounding community about what they know about the family. Gather all the information you need to make a sound judgement about whether it is a smart move to marry into this family. Consider your options carefully and do not sign up for more than you can handle.

8. Should I reject someone who wants me to live with their family?

Not necessarily. First find out what the living arrangements would be.

Will you have an entire floor in the house to yourself? Will the family intervene in your private affairs, or will they keep a healthy distance? Is it a long-term setup or something short-term?

Don't reject a potential spouse based on your fears of living with your in-laws. Ask questions about the proposed arrangements, get to know the family better, and then make your decision based on what you know you can personally handle.

9. How can I be certain the person is not lying to me?

Choosing a spouse is always a risk. Take the means to protect yourself from being cheated.

- Ask serious questions and assess their character.

- Contact their references and do your research about how others would describe this person.

- Do not ignore any red flags or troubling signs.

- Resolve any trust issues that you may have, which could impact your outlook.

Most importantly, make *du'ā'* to Allāh Most High to protect you from harm and guide you to the best decision for your worldly and next-wordly life *inshā'Allāh.*

10. It is taking a long time to find someone. What do I do if I feel like giving up?

Many people experience ups and downs during their search. For some, it may take years of searching before settling on a person. Try to focus on what truly matters.

Firstly, rejoice in the fact that Allāh Most High is guiding you to obey Him by seeking marriage instead of indulging in unlawful relationships. Your efforts will be written in your book of good deeds *inshā'Allāh*.

Moreover, use this as an opportunity to grow in your faith. Practice placing your trust in Allāh Most High (*tawakkul*) and being content with the idea that He is in control. He will give you what is best for you at the time that is best for you.

Allāh Most High says, "Say: 'Nothing will ever befall us except what Allāh has destined for us. He is our Protector.' So in Allāh let the believers place their trust." (*al-Tawba*, 9:51)

Affirm your conviction in being satisfied with His decree (*qadr*), including the good and the bad. Remember that you will be rewarded for your patience.

Lastly, ask Allāh Most High to make the process easy and quick. Sometimes hardships are sent as a test for you to turn to Allāh alone and call upon Him. He loves to see your neediness.

Allāh Most High says:

> **"And when My servants ask you (O Muhammad) concerning Me, indeed I am near. I respond to the invocation of the supplicant when he calls upon Me. So let them respond to Me (in obedience) and believe in Me, so that they may be guided....."**

(*al-Baqara*, 2:186)

May Allāh Most High give you ease and success (*tawfiq*) with choosing your other half.

100+ POTENTIAL SPOUSE QUESTIONS

www.muslimmarriagecoach.com/
potential-spouse-questions

SIGN UP FOR OUR PREMARITAL COACHING PROGRAM

www.muslimmarriagecoach.com/
premarital-coaching

Appendix

About the Authors

Naielah Ackbarali is the founder and CEO of Muslima Coaching. She studied various Islamic sciences with top traditional scholars in both Syria and Jordan for over 15 years. She is currently continuing her advanced Islamic studies in England.

Naielah is a trained strategic relationship coach, certified life coach, and a certified NLP Master Practitioner. Combined with her knowledge from Islamic studies, coaching experience, and personal marriage of more than 16 years, she offers faith-based marriage coaching to couples, wives, and singles.

She is an author of several books on marriage and menstruation, and she has been featured on the Islam Channel and British Muslim TV.

Anas Sillwood is a convert to Islam, an international businessman, a student of the Islamic sciences, and a certified professional life coach. He is the founder of SHUKR clothing, the first modest and Islamic clothing company in the West.

He studied various Islamic sciences with reputable scholars in both Jordan and Syria for over 20 years and is currently continuing his advanced Islamic studies in England.

Combining his worldly knowledge, Islamic studies, coaching experience, and personal marriage of more than

16 years, he offers faith-based singles and marriage coaching to Muslim men. He has also been featured on the Islam Channel and Iqra TV.

Find them at their marriage coaching website!

muslim marriage coach

www.muslimmarriagecoach.com

Printed in Great Britain
by Amazon

42590042R00098